BLIMEY!

From Bohemia to Britpop: The London Artworld from Francis Bacon to Damien Hirst

Matthew Collings

Ian MacMillan
18·3·97 3·39pm.

Matthew Collings
3.40pm   18.3.97

Modern British

Quo Vadis exterior Dean Street London

Hello Reader!

I went to Quo Vadis the other night. That's the well-known restaurant in Dean Street that Damien Hirst recently redesigned. Now it's full of art by young people who are in *Vogue* and on TV all the time. Are they any good? How long will it last? Is it just a little twisted branch off the main trunk of art, or is it the main trunk, like Cézanne and Rembrandt? Is it like Rock music only more soulful? Why isn't Damien Hirst soulful then? Who's it made for? Why do they do it? We know why Rock is made, because there's a huge popular demand for it. But there's no popular demand for contemporary art. Although there is a popular fascination with it nowadays. It's in Benson & Hedges ads and in Rock promo videos and TV ads. There's one where a teenager makes a sandwich that he fantasizes is a work of art, and the next thing you know it's in a vitrine in a white gallery with intellectuals peering at it.

Quo Vadis interior

Behind where I was sitting having my Martini off a table top with a tungsten light shining through it, so it was hard to look down at your twiglets and olives without being blinded, there were two vitrines, one boy-blue, one girl-pink, each with a partly flayed cow's head in it. A bit further back there was a glass cabinet with shelves lined with surgical instruments. Around me, the walls were painted handsome muted purples and greys. On them there was a painting of some cigarette butts, a photo of the artist Sarah Lucas staring blankly, smoking a cigarette, and a painting by the American artist, Sean Landers, of some clowns in a rowing boat on storm-tossed waves.

I went downstairs for the food, which was Modern British, designed by Marco Pierre White, the most famous chef, who is always being photographed looking violent, holding a meat cleaver. In front of me, there was a bronze chimp by Sean Landers. Everyone felt fine. Straight-looking types in dark suits ordered their meals on expenses for themselves and their partners and personal assistants. I started thinking about the past.

Mighty Baby

Mother Rachel! Mother Rachel! That's the cry I remember going up in the middle of the night from the kitchen at 93 Oakley Street, Chelsea. It was the Glasgow poet Eddie Linden, drunk, with red hair, frightening the unmarried mothers. There were always lots of them there. My own mother was one of them. We used to sit in a circle of mothers watching the black and white TV. *The Wednesday Play* or *The Virginian* or *All Our Yesterdays*.

It was a permanently shabby kitchen. The walls were yellow and there was red lino on the floor. There was a Sellotaped collage of magazine photos from the Sunday papers almost covering one wall. Starving Africans. David Hockney's *Tired Indians*. Over and in between the pictures were pencilled and felt-penned phone numbers, and slogans from the writings of R.D.Laing.

Rachel Pinney, who ran the house, was a psychiatrist and a campaigner for world peace. This was the last of the several homes she used to own. She had made it into a shore for the lost and drifting to wash up on, for £3 and £5 a week rent. Eddie Linden wasn't really her son, any more than I was. He had been one of her patients. He was just drunk and raving and had washed up here briefly. Her real son had been hitch-hiking in Israel, so news reports about the Six Day War was another thing we used to watch. I passed through here every weekend between the ages of six and thirteen, when I lived in a council-run children's home in St Mary's Cray, in Orpington. I came to Chelsea on the train on Fridays and returned to the home on Sunday evenings.

All sorts passed through. Peace campaigners, patients, doctors, shaky people who'd had electric shock treatment. Sometimes Quentin Crisp came round, with blue hair, to play chess. Dust was piled up thickly in his flat across the road in Oakley Gardens.

Later, when it was the end of the 60s, the mothers drifted away and the place filled up with members of Rock bands. The Family, who recorded an instrumental named after the house, *93's OK J*, and the lesser known Mighty Baby, who had been to India. They sat in their rooms, wearing their afghans and afros and snakeskin boots, and listening to

Neil Young's *Cinnamon Girl*, or Frank Zappa's *Peaches En Regalia*, eating lychees.

Rachel, who tolerated the rockers and took their rent – which was now up to £5 and £10 a week – but didn't socialize with them because she didn't understand them and was afraid of their drugs, ate bankrupt soup.

That was her name for it. It was what the kitchen always smelt of. It was an army-sized tureen of old vegetables and slightly off meat that she would just add to now and then, and reheat, until some mother or band member or other couldn't bear the smell any longer and would throw it away. But then, horribly, it would start up again.

The Mounties

For the cause of world peace she didn't talk on Wednesdays. She would just write things down on a piece of paper. I'm afraid the answer is No. Or, Where are my glasses? Once she allowed an autistic child to cut all her hair off with nail scissors and for a few weeks she had a radical ragged grey prison haircut instead of her normal severe lesbian do.

But then she really did go to prison, for six months in 1970, for kidnapping me when I was fourteen. She gave me some money to run away to Canada. Some detectives arrested me there after a month and when I was brought back to London, by a London detective and a WPC who had come out to get me, it turned out Interpol, the FBI, Scotland Yard and the Mounties had all been in on the search.

The Bohemians

People who are in the artworld get there by all sorts of different springboards. For some of them it is a step up the social ladder, from working class to middle class. But some of course are born into that class. I was born into the Bohemian class, which is a branch of the middle class. My mother went to art school and then later on taught art in secondary schools. Her mother was a dancer and her father distributed films in South America for J. Arthur Rank.

WOMAN IN MATTHEW QUIZ

DOLORES FABIAN, 34, is pictured in London yesterday after spending seven hours at Chelsea police station helping police with enquiries into the disappearance of 14-year-old Matthew Collings.

Miss Fabian lives in the same house in Oakley Street, Chelsea, as Dr. Rachel Pliney, 60, who was charged last week with kidnapping Matthew. Matthew, son of a

Chelsea schoolteacher is now believed to be in North America.

Miss Fabian, an artist and writer who also sings said last night: "I honestly did not want to be involved, I dare not say anything because there are so many involved."

Under the name Fabian she has painted Richard Burton, Sir Laurence Olivier, and Mick Jagger.

Kensington and Chelsea Post
April 1970

Weeping

After I was kidnapped I was sent to a therapeutic community in Kent, and when I left I did some manual labouring jobs for two years, which were very tiring, like refuse-collecting, cleaning at the British Museum, putting up Residents Only parking signs and mixing concrete.

And then I went to The Byam Shaw School of Painting, where my mother had been when she was fifteen. It was the 1970s. I studied the art magazines in the library and learned to recognize works by contemporary New York artists like Mel Bochner and Lawrence Weiner. They did diagrams of triangles on the floor made of pebbles or lengths of tape, and words on the wall that said things like Eight Pints of White Paint. Then I bought a book called *Six Years*. It documented in awesome detail six years' worth of Conceptual art. From 1966 to 1972.

There were the early sayings of Gilbert & George, which went something like, Art we only wish to serve you. And the first Conceptual art manifestos by Joseph Kosuth. There were photos of cooling towers and mounds of earth in the desert, and Robert Smithson's *Spiral Jetty* photographed from the air, and a woman weeping.

Art & Language

A man came to the school and gave us a lecture about Art & Language. They were an international art group, spread all over the world, in New York, Australia and Oxford. They typed the letter A in the middle of a sheet of paper, and then after that one of them left, because it was only formalism, which was a bit confusing because we'd just got used to the idea that formalism was minimalism.

One second

We went to exhibitions in Cork Street and at the ICA, in The Mall. We saw colour field paintings in acrylic by John Hoyland, and some suitcases and railway sleepers by a Greek Conceptual artist. At the Tate Gallery we saw a John Latham retrospective. He burned books and made one-second drawings done with spattered ink. And at the Serpentine Gallery we saw a Howard Hodgkin retrospective. He painted dots and patterns and abstract figures who were always in restaurants.

John Hoyland

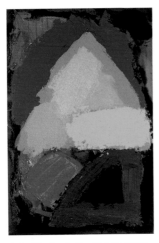

John Hoyland *Trespassers* 1982

Space

Also at the art school I learned about space, which we had to paint and draw in life classes. The naked models stood or lay around in set-ups with easels and draped sheets and pieces of coloured paper, to make the space richer, with the daylight streaming in through big grid-shaped windows.

We had to draw or paint the scenes with a ruthless spatial eye. Not first of all putting the model's eyes, nose, ears and mouth, or nipples, in the middle of the paper or canvas, with a very sharp pencil or tiny sable brush, as we would very much like to have done, and as we all certainly did on our first morning's life class when we started at the school. But instead blocking in the big areas first, not caring if it was an arm or an easel or a window or a door or the side of the head of the student in front of us. And then gradually getting all the shapes to relate together, so a convincing space would appear.

We would go on from there, blocking in smaller and smaller shapes and going back and correcting the big ones. And then somewhere in all that blocking, after many hours or days, there would be the naked model rendered at last, all dots and dashes and wobbly squares and rectangles and negative shapes, in rugged thick black charcoal or 6B pencil outlines, looking like a wonky diagram of a human.

Or if it was a painting, the lines and shapes would be in thick rich mixed-up oil colours, every contour the result of endless other contours shuffling and colliding, and the model would look like a poor hot and cold coloured paint creature, glowing from a nuclear explosion.

They hate me

One day in the 1980s I was standing outside one of the many Waddington galleries that existed in those days, with Julian Schnabel, who was having an exhibition in at least two of them. I looked down the road and saw John Hoyland and Mick Moon coming towards us. At that time they still showed at Waddington's. Schnabel was in his early thirties and his paintings, which were enormous and made of velvet and linoleum and smashed plates and antlers and oil paint and wax, cost $100,000 each. They were figurative and abstract and flat and sculptural and camp and butch, all at the same time. They were always being photographed and written and talked about. They were attacked for being loud and brutish. Or praised for being full of depth and mystery as well as loud and brutish.

Julian Schnabel

The poor English artists getting nearer and nearer to us now only did a pleasing decorative, sympathetic, but not aggressively innovative type of flat abstract painting, using masking tape. They were influenced by Matisse, who said he wanted art to be like a comfortable armchair for a tired businessman to rest in.

In the 70s the artists who did this type of abstract art had been menaced by Conceptual art and Minimalism, which had institutional support and had become the official academy. It was always in exhibitions at the Tate gallery and the Hayward gallery. The abstract painters wanted painting to come back. But their idea of painting was something like the old Abstract Expressionism of the 50s, but a later smoother version. Abstract Expressionism without tears, more designed and handsome and adjusted than the original kind. The orignal kind always had a rhetoric of tragedy and anguish and Existentialism and psychoanalysis attached to it.

Julian Schnabel
A Motherfucker 1983

The Conceptual and Minimal academy artists laughed at what they saw as the hopeless formalism – which was always something that anybody could laugh at when they were unclear about what was happening – of the abstract painting stream. Ha ha, they went.

But both sides got a surprise when Schnabel arrived. Naturally Post-Modern, he laughed at Conceptual art and formalism as well and just did whatever he liked. He was Mister Smart in about 1978 and then Mister Huge. We don't talk about him so much in the 90s, because his particular brand of iconoclasm seems standard now. But he was the first monster superbrat of the 80s artworld, the model for Jeff Koons, and then, later, Damien Hirst.

But anyway, the two English artists now approaching Waddington's didn't have a press image or any controversy attached to them. Except that they had been in a war in the 70s, the war between muralists and abstractionists. The muralists were old-fashioned socialists whose response to the confusion of the times was that they wanted art to be murals on the Westway, depicting Work, or Trade Union banners. The abstract artists wanted art to be timeless, and certainly above socialism. But it was such a remote little mild skirmish that within the London art-world it was barely a memory now, and everywhere else it was just a void.

So when the two abstract painters came right up to Schnabel, standing on the corner outside their old gallery which was now taken over by Post-Modernism, it was like an allegory, like that painting by Courbet called *Bonjour Monsieur Courbet*, where Courbet is standing in front of a gate and someone is greeting him, and it's like the arrival of something new.

But agreeable as they were, the two painters didn't say Bonjour Monsieur Schnabel you bastard, why do we still struggle while you glide effortlessly to the top with your jazzy ideas? Instead they greeted him brightly and said Hi! And he greeted them the same way in return. And when they passed he said, *sotto voce*, with a *c'est la vie* half smile, what was probably true, and with good reason, I suppose – They hate my guts.

Minimalism

Another time I went to an afternoon press opening at the Saatchi Gallery for an exhibition of vast imposing rusted-metal Minimal sculptures by Richard Serra. He was over from America and he was angry with everyone because *Artforum*, the most important art magazine, would not defend him over the *Tilted Arc* controversy, when his hundreds of yards long rusted-metal public sculpture by that name was removed from a plaza somewhere because the local office workers resented having to walk round it to look for a place to eat sandwiches at lunchtime. When he found

Damien Hirst

out I was the editor of an art magazine, he began to rage bitterly and said he was going to sue the government. He said the only real concern of art magazines nowadays was advertising revenue. Then later there was a dinner at a restaurant and he said he saw his best friends die for art, including Robert Smithson. He leaned across Sarah Kent, the art critic, and held an empty bottle up to me. If you were in New York right now, he said, you'd get this round your head. It went on like that until I had to leave, and although he kindly or diplomatically phoned up the magazine the next day to apologize, I still can't help thinking that perhaps it goes on raging like that in his mind all the time. Even though nobody cares what his sculptures used to mean. Only what they used to look like, so they can be recycled as parody Minimalism. Or his old films of himself throwing molten lead at the floor.

Warehouse shows

The 1980s saw the rise of Young British art. The first thing was a series of group shows held in warehouse spaces. These shows were called things like 'Freeze', 'Modern Medicine', 'Gambler', or 'East Country Yard Show'. Meaningless titles which have now entered legend. The art wasn't all that different from anything that had been seen before. But the exhibitions were very professionally organized. Even though they

'Freeze' 1988
works by **Simon Patterson** and **Damien Hirst**

were only put on by students, or recently graduated students, they had a bold European *Kunsthalle* look, or SoHo in New York look, or pages of *Flash Art* or *Artforum* look.

666

The main personality to come out of the warehouse shows was Damien Hirst. In the exhibition called 'Gambler', which was a little bit after 'Freeze', he showed a sculpture that was two six-feet-square glass cases next to each other, connected by a circular hole. Vitrines. They looked like recycled Minimalism, which was quite normal for the time.

But inside the vitrines was a less standard sight. There were flies and maggots in there. And a severed cow's head. There was an ultraviolet light insect-o-cutor as well. There was a little natural life cycle going on. You could imagine the cycle happening: the maggots hatching, the flies flying around and having fly sex and laying more eggs in the head, and the new flies doing the same, and all of them getting electrocuted in the end. It was called *A Hundred Years* and later he did another one called *A Thousand Years*.

Damien Hirst *A Thousand Years* 1990

A good idea

Clearly it was a good idea. The vitrines looked like Minimalism in the sense that they looked like the parodies of 60s Minimalism that were going on a lot in the art of the 80s. But the flies were a twist in a different direction. The idea with the normal Minimalism parodies of the 80s was to re-do 60s Minimalism in a formally impure way that went against the essence of the original movement, which was to be utterly pure, but retained its handsome look. So the parody Minimalism was supposed to be critical in some way. Critical of art or life or society. Whatever. You went around frowning and saying Hmm, yes, that's very interesting, it's critical.

But this impurity of flies was so fantastically impure, through still perfectly chiming with another 60s art tendency, process art, and another, truth to materials art, that the whole thing seemed not just correct and à la mode. It seemed correct and à la mode but a bit hilariously silly and gruesome and theatrical and new and endlessly poetically metaphoric and expressive, as well.

Influence of Sean Landers

A lot of the art you see in London by young artists of the 90s is half coherent illiterate rambling thoughts that the young artist just writes down in biro or in clumsy typewriting, and somehow it's art. Cartoony doodles and scribbles, thought balloons, biro ventings saying, I am a cunt. In an abject neo-Punk, rage against impotence kind of way. Or frank embracing of impotence. You can't tell which it is.

When you think about the older artists going around in their suits and being in biennales and giving the same interviews all the time about their concerns and being a bit gratingly half-intellectual, you feel refreshed by this frankly abject juvenile style, even if it's only for a moment.

The New York slacker artist Sean Landers, who does rambling semi-jokey confessional writings on canvas, is a main innovator of abjection. Some of his writings canvases were part of one of Saatchi's exhibition of his new acquisitions of young American art. Everything else in the

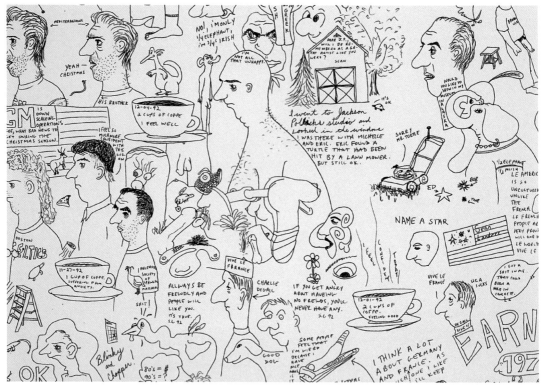

Sean Landers
I'm Nailed Right In (detail)
1993

show was the usual fare. You recognized it was art, but there was nothing else interesting about it. But Sean Landers' writings are really worth reading because they're so funny. It just seems by the by that they're art.

I was interviewing him once and he was laughing about his use of a live chimpanzee in one of his video works, and when I asked him if his art was meant to provoke, he said, Well at least he hadn't sawed the monkey in half and put it in formaldehyde.

One thing that emerged from this interview is that nobody has given a label to the mood of the international artworld today, now that the mood has moved on from political correctness, which reached its height in about 1992. Young artists are just naturally politically correct now, because they never were anything else. So their art can be free of correctness in the sense of correctness being the main statement. They just think they are correct in their lives so that frees their art.

Good thinking young artists! And they don't feel any pressure to read anything hard any more, like social theory books or investigations into the structure of language.

Sean Landers says he feels he might have been a pioneer on the trail of everybody not reading anything they wouldn't naturally want to read any more. In his recently published first book, which is called (*sic*), a joke on his own bad spelling, he tells a lot of very engaging stories about lying in bed and listening to soft Rock with girlfriends instead of working. The many spelling errors of the original manuscript are retained, so that threw is spelt through, and hetero, hedero, and fiercely, fearsly.

It's hard to read at first but once drawn in you find yourself wondering why all books aren't written like that, and you think that's what Cubism was probably like at first.

Niel Sedacka was so right, he writes at one point, *Breakeing up is hard to do. Every time I break up with a woman it makes me want to kick that bloated fat wheasle in the balls.*

Bob and Roberta Smith *Probable* 1993

So whereas in the past a work of art almost couldn't be taken seriously if it didn't have cubist fragmentation and flatness, or if it didn't have drips, or if it wasn't a photo of some pebbles – the equivalent now is if it isn't scribbled casually in biro and doesn't have a slightly unhinged air of negativity and world-weary black humour, and seeing the black heart in everything, but at the same time being in an oceanic sea of oneness with ordinary people and their obsession with pop culture and street fashion and the movies.

Silk Cuts

It soon went around that Charles Saatchi had bought that flies sculpture, and after that you would always hear about Damien Hirst in connection with Saatchi. Saatchi had given him an idea for this, or told him to do that, and so on.

Damien Hirst *The Acquired Inability to Escape* 1991

One thing he perhaps told him to do, or gave him the idea for, was a vitrine huge enough to have an executive style desk and chair inside it, with a lot of space round the objects, enough for a person to walk in and sit down, except that the vitrine was completely sealed. On the desk was a packet of Silk Cut cigarettes and an ashtray full of butts. It was handsome and ugly at the same time. It was as good as the flies, but different. They both seemed to be about bringing back the old heavy contents of art but still being smart, clever and emotionally disengaged. Of course nowadays we wonder if we really care for that emotionally disengaged sense as much as we used to.

The meaning of vitrines

Unexpected things in vitrines became his style. As well as the big boxes and cubes of 60s Minimalism, vitrines recalled Joseph Beuys. Joseph Beuys, who died in 1986, was the opposite of Minimalism. Minimalism was the *ne plus ultra* of formalism, and the last moment of High Modernism, whereas Joseph Beuys was an anti-formalist and one of the innovators of a far out branch of Modernism that eventually became Post-Modernism. But by the 80s it was all the same. It could all be used again differently to make new parody art.

Nothing

Without the imposing, Minimal sculpture-like vitrine, with its sheet glass sides and heavy steel edges, the Silk Cuts artwork would have looked a bit nothing. Nowadays, in the 90s, the nothing look would be good. Today someone else might easily do the Silk Cuts and ashtray without the vitrine, and everybody would be able to tell it was still some kind of art. In fact I might do it myself. But in those days there was a different mood.

His titles were all good

The Silk Cuts vitrine sculpture was called *The Acquired Inability to Escape*. All his works had good titles. Once he showed a ping-pong ball suspended on a jet of air that had a title that was like a track from a record by Primal Scream. Or the name of a rave off the M25 Orbital in 1988. *I want to spend the rest of my life with everyone everywhere, one to one, always forever now* 1991. As well as vitrines he did paintings of aimless coloured dots. After he had been doing them for a while, he started giving them titles from the listings in pharmaceutical drugs catalogues. When he did some glass shelves with packets of medicine on them, the shelves all had titles adapted from songs by The Sex Pistols. Nowadays records and raves all have titles that are like works by Damien Hirst.

Maybe

Maybe Saatchi told him to do *The Physical Impossibility of Death in the Mind of Someone Living*. I don't know. But I was on the lawn outside the Serpentine Gallery one summer evening – it was the opening for 'Broken English', another Conceptual and Minimal parody kind of

Damien Hirst *The Physical Impossibility of Death in the Mind of Someone Living* 1991

Freeze catalogue

show – when someone mentioned that Damien Hirst was going to be suspending a shark in formaldehyde and it was going to cost £50,000 or £12,000, or some very high figure, and Saatchi was paying. For a long time before this work was eventually seen it was already known about. When it was finally shown it didn't look any different from how you'd imagined it. So it was hard to think about it seriously. But that was at the Saatchi Gallery a bit later on, after the first spate of warehouse shows.

Freeze

Of course warehouse shows are still going on. In fact there are thousands of them. But it's a different thing now, it's not new any more. 'Freeze', the first one, was organized by Damien Hirst. He didn't have anything in it that was of any interest, or that anyone noticed or talked about much. Just some painted cardboard construction things. He wasn't much good at art at first. Or at least, he seemed to put his main energy into curating. It was only later on that he suddenly seemed to be very good at actual art. But then you started to hear about his early collages at art school, which he made out of bits of *bric-a-brac* he found in an abandoned house somewhere. And the idea that 'Freeze' was also a kind of collage, only of other people's art, started to take hold in artworld mythology. And so the whole notion of his curating activity started to get a special magic art-like glow around it.

Not oppressed

Part of the mythology of the Young British artists is that they were oppressed by Thatcher's Britain and were rebels against the dominant culture. But sometimes people argue the opposite, that being enterprising and entrepreneurial and putting on luxury entertainment exhibitions in spaces that were previously warehouses but had become available because of the recession is not really revolutionary.

For 'Freeze', Damien Hirst got hold of some gallery mailing lists, which isn't a hard thing to do, it's just not something a lot of students would have thought of then. So he did it and consequently quite illustrious art people, like Norman Rosenthal from the Royal Academy and Nicholas Serota from the Tate Gallery, and some collectors, and some curators and critics and private gallerists – more art culture sub-groupings not exactly known for their revolutionariness – all came to the exhibition.

He also organized a professional looking catalogue with an articulate, smooth (that is, impossible to either disagree or agree with) essay in it by an established art critic. Again, this isn't an impossibly hard thing to organize. But at that time young artists weren't thinking that you simply had to have a professional looking catalogue and a gallery mailing list to make an exhibition seem real.

Not being a mollusc

In fact you might have argued that the whole point of a self-help show outside the main system of galleries would be to cut through the official ritual of exhibiting and do something a bit more straightforward and pure. And indeed artists' self-help shows until this point had been about exactly that. But nobody paid much attention to them, as these exhibitions were just poor defenseless molluscs out of their shells.

Uptight

So this 'Freeze' event was definitely a change of attitude. The new approach came from the artists' awareness of the hyper-professional world of international art. Or at least the illusion of hyper-professionalism that the international artworld tried in those days to maintain at all times. Art wasn't about being in a studio creating. It was about being in a studio creating and then being in a smart white gallery and having a catalogue and reviews in art magazines and flying to different international art spots and having curators and professional uptight zombies of the artworld suck up to you briefly.

Even having a studio wasn't all that important. The other things were really important. But it's true you had to have some creativity, you couldn't just do the whole thing on nothing. Although with Damien Hirst it did seem at first that nothing was pretty much all he was going on. But this was part of the thrill for many. It was his cheekiness.

Mere detail

As well as his cardboard things, he was painting coloured dots directly on the wall that looked like the paintings of the German artist Gerhard Richter. Later he started doing them on canvas. He had lots of jars of mixed-up colours and he would draw out the circles with a pencil, in a simple grid, using a compass, and then fill them in more or less arbitrarily, with a different colour in each circle. Or get someone else to do it.

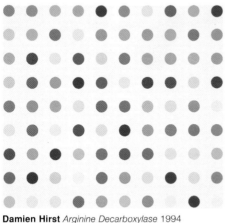

Damien Hirst *Arginine Decarboxylase* 1994

Gerhard Richter, who was already well known in West Germany in the 60s and was an international super-star by the 80s, was famous for doing a kind of abstract painting that refused all contents or meanings that seemed remotely soppy. All his contents and meanings were in the hardcore nihilism range. Among other things, he painted enormous colour charts, with thousands of different shades in neat rectangles separated by white space. They looked like commercial colour charts, only hugely enlarged. It was these Richters that Damien Hirst's dots were like. Aimless but somehow piercing and right.

Paradoxically, considering the hardness of Richter's content, there is a silliness and pretentiousness to the whole Richter cult, that can be unbearable. He attracts lobotomy zombie adulation like nobody's business. And it must be said, the same goes for the Damien Hirst cult. But in his defense, Damien Hirst is always lively and normal-seeming as a person, both in ordinary life and in official public appearances. Whereas Richter in the same situations is quite dreary and vain and makes you feel really unsympathetic towards him and tired of art.

But all this is mere detail to the warehouse story. It didn't really matter what bits of meaning-static clung to the international art objects that the warehouse artists emulated. The point was to recycle them ruthlessly and make them work in this new strange context. The London context. London had been terrible, it was provincial and ghastly. The only good thing it had then was art schools.

Drinking
with criminals

Art schools

Hardly any artists we ever hear about didn't go to art school. Francis Bacon is the most famous exception. He designed furniture in the 30s, then he did some paintings and the art critic Herbert Read saw one and thought it was good. Then he went back to not doing them again, until 1945 when he did the triptych in the Tate Gallery called *Three Studies for Figures at the Base of a Crucifixion*. Everyone praised it and said the triffid-like monster figures were like the Eumenides from Greek tragedy, and that's when he started really painting seriously and consistently. But he always seemed quite proud of never having studied art formally. That's not surprising when you think that at the time he would have gone to art school, art in Britain was quite boring. He shocked the teachers at the Royal College once when he agreed to do some painting there for a while so everyone could see how he worked, because it seemed very messy and extravagant with a lot of expensive colours, and he cut reproductions out of expensive library books for reference.

Lucian Freud almost didn't go to art school either, but he did a few classes at the Central School, so he didn't totally not go, like Francis Bacon.

Rigour and writhing

The art schools all had their different atmospheres. For example, Slade figurative painting was all rigorous dots and dashes. These marks were the pictorial scaffolding and they showed exactly where everything should be, so there was no chance of the subject escaping. Whereas Camberwell figurative painting was brushy and loose, with the subject writhing freely.

Sir William Coldstream invented that measuring style they did at the Slade. He helped start the Euston Road School, which was a real school in Euston Road in the 1930s, but which we have come to think of loosely as a school in the art history sense, like the New York School, or *Ecole de Paris*. It means urban drab realism scenes. It has always stood for a kind of anti-arty high moral fibre, with no mucking about. It has a kind of world view that says everything went wrong with Picasso, but before that – with Cézanne especially – everything was good.

But in the 80s a lot of the art schools were merged together into a single institution called The London Institute, and as a result the individual atmospheres were lost.

Splendid

A great campaigner against the merging was the painter and writer Patrick Heron, who is a kind of peacock figure, very splendid looking but with an unexpected high warbly voice and a laughing enthusiastic self-confident talking style that could easily be mistaken for theatrical or camp. But his campaigning letters to the press were full of passion and he really did believe that art schools in Britain were the best in the world.

In the past Patrick Heron had campaigned against the idea that stripes in Modern Art came from New York. They really came from Cornwall, he said, which is where he lives. But it was harder to get worked up about that issue.

The Sirs

In the 60s, the art schools all introduced complementary studies, which meant the study of art history and ideas about art, or things relating to art. Which after a while it turned out could be anything at all. So part of the time you learned practice and part of the time you learned theory. It was Sir William Coldstream who thought of this first, in 1961, when he introduced the concept of the Diploma in Art and Design into art school education. The Dip. A.D.

It's great when artists are knights. It'll be great when we have Sir Damien Hirst and Sir Douglas Gordon and Dame Gillian Wearing.

Goldsmiths

Today most art schools still have different departments for different media. The sculpture department, the painting department, the printing department and so on. One main exception is Goldsmiths College, where they just join up all the departments and you don't specialize because it's all creativity. That's where I went in 1990, to do the MA course there, and I can really recommend it.

Goldsmiths is where the warehouse artists mostly went, in the 80s. Their teachers were Michael Craig Martin and Jon Thompson. Michael Craig Martin is very media-friendly and often turns up in style magazines and on TV. Jon Thompson was considered a bit more theory-obsessive and intellectual and professorial, and rarely appeared on TV, except for one memorable late night discussion programme called *Voices*, where he must have confused even the late night audience with his talk of the atomization of contemporary existence. But they were both good. And so were the other teachers there. The main other ones were Gerard Hemsworth and Nick de Ville. Nick de Ville has a particularly sexy name which is only right because he designed some record covers for Roxy Music in the 70s.

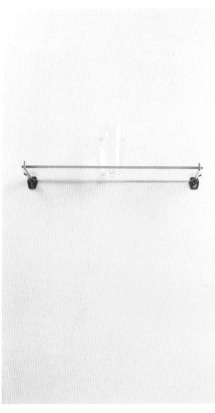

Michael Craig-Martin *An Oak Tree* (detail) 1973

Don't teach there

One noticeable quirk of young Goldsmiths artists is that they tend to put down the courses there and the teachers, and try and cultivate a sense of their art having arrived by auto-genesis, out of nowhere, as if by magic. So it's a thankless task to be the teacher of a star.

Not punished

It's true that life painting in art schools is more or less out now. You could easily go through your art school years today without doing one. But it's not true that you would actually be encouraged to never do one, or punished if you secretly did one.

Some of the other artists

Some of the other artists in 'Freeze' did more substantial looking things than Damien Hirst's constructions. But it turned out their substance was in the wrong direction. His initial slightness was absolutely right because it meant he had less baggage to throw out later on, and there was more room for good new things.

Ian Davenport did big dripping paintings that looked absurdly like Jackson Pollock, but with special new 80s weightlessness. And Fiona Rae did things that looked like parody formalism of the colourful abstract painting kind. Abstract blobs and marks and drips and cartoon shapes that assembled into funny hieroglyphs, neatly laid out in rows. The overall neatness excitingly contradicting the freeness of the individual marks.

Neither of them looked any more than the normal art you would see in New York at that time by earnest new young painters who would get a review in *Art in America* or *Artforum*. But not make a particular stir because there was too much other art around that looked like that.

And some of the other artists did installations and photos which also looked a bit Cologne/New York international normal style. This style was to re-do the Conceptual art forms – photos and slides and so on – of the 60s and 70s, but with new mystery content. Not the old boring content of the class struggle, or Wittgenstein, or whatever.

Friendly Freeze

So these first warehouse shows were not revolutionary or rebellious or anarchic or crazy or unbelievable, they were quite conventional in a way. The aim was not to buck the system but to get into it absolutely as soon as possible by showing how utterly system-friendly your art was.

Above: **Ian Davenport** *Untitled* 1988
Below: **Fiona Rae** *Untitled (breathe)* 1997

Quickly

So quite quickly the established galleries started taking on the new artists. There were little and medium-size galleries who took them on, but also huge ones. The first big news wasn't Damien Hirst but Ian Davenport, who was taken on by Leslie Waddington.

At that time Waddington still had a lot of spaces on Cork Street and was considered a very powerful dealer. It was even more odd that he should have taken on Ian Davenport than if the other two big powerful galleries, Anthony d'Offay or the Lisson gallery, had taken him on, because Waddington isn't particularly associated with really trendy art. He shows safe blue-chip Modernism, like Picasso, or market proved contemporary international stars like Schnabel. Or the German artist Georg Baselitz's upside-down paintings.

So Ian Davenport went from being a student to being a safe blue-chip investment in about half an hour. The story went around that Michael Craig Martin, who showed at Waddington's, and who had famously exhibited a glass of water in the 70s and said it was an oak tree, had introduced Leslie Waddington to Ian Davenport's work and Waddington had taken Ian Davenport on and the arrangement was that he should be on a retainer of £25,000 a year. It was fabulous, exciting gossip, much better than the usual gossip of those times which was only about Arts Council Grants, or who had got a teaching job or a new studio or switched from acrylics to oils.

But his paintings were close to the old post-Abstract Expressionism smoothed-out abstract designer style, and after a while they got even closer to that and a bit too handsomely streamlined, and finally they weren't talked about much any more. Maybe they were good. Maybe not. No one cared. But that's moving on a bit from the warehouse explosion.

Soon after Ian Davenport was taken on, Waddington took on Fiona Rae, who also gradually merged back into the ordinary stream of art. Her paintings got more and more confident and bold and packed, and more loopy and dare-devil, and the simple underlying grid structures were dropped in favour of less obvious, more ambitious and complicated structures. And although they also remain close today to post-Abstract Expressionism emptiness, and are a bit formalist at heart, they go on looking quite lively.

Formalism

After all, is it so bad? What is it anyway? Nobody knows.

£500

One of the artists in 'Freeze' exhibited some light bulbs that blinked on and off. There was a TV programme about the show, and to give an impression of the 'Freeze' artists' professionalism the producers of the programme arranged for this artist, Angela Bulloch, and her dealer, Maureen Paley, to have a discussion about the cost of the light bulbs. How much will you be selling it for? asked Angela Bulloch. £500, said the dealer.

Not talked about

Interestingly, a whole stream of painting rose up around this time that followed the Ian Davenport aesthetic. New young painters did deliberately empty paintings that emphasized the process of how they were made, maybe with lots of masking tape and straight lines, or something like that, and they went on doing them even though nobody talked about them.

One of these is Jason Martin, who gets a very wide brush, as wide as the canvas he is going to paint on, which might be ten feet wide for example, and then kind of screeds a load of paint across it in one go. When you see one you think, Well, I probably wouldn't have thought of doing that. Another one is Peter Davies, who does a lot of straight lines with masking tape that cross over each other. And two others are Zebedee Jones and Clem Crosby, who both do built-up surfaces of oil paint that they just pile on.

Love

After flies Damien Hirst did butterflies. That was in an exhibition called 'In and Out of Love' which was held on two floors of a temporary space somewhere in the West End. The atmosphere was kept humid because that's how butterflies like it. Upstairs they were alive, flying around, with bowls of sugared water laid out on tables for them to drink from. Sometimes they settled on the bare white surfaces of some canvases on the walls which had rows of plants on shelves running along the bottom edge of the canvases. Downstairs they were dead, stuck to the surfaces of bright-coloured gloss paint monochrome Minimal parody paintings. Down here instead of sugared water there were ashtrays on tables loaded with butts. It was creepy having the butterflies flying around you. But not as bad as that butterfly place near Kew Gardens where it seems all right at first but then they start settling horribly on your trouser leg and it's like being in a nightmare.

Francis Bacon and Young British art

Until the 60s the London artworld was ghastly except for Francis Bacon. Then it was a bit more exciting for a while, with Pop Art, but it soon sank back into boredom, until the late 80s when Young British art began. This is largely, because of the nature of the art system in Britain, a London-based movement. When it began, this movement was a local phenomenon only. Outside this country nothing about it would have looked out of the ordinary. But then gradually art everywhere else became incredibly slight and sank down to the level of the new British art. Because the London artists seemed lively and motivated and definitely going forwards, when everyone else was confused and going round in circles, everyone in the other countries agreed to pretend London was more exciting than it really was, and started having shows of British invasion art, and putting it in all the magazines. It was a London youth-quake. So by now we all really think that the London artworld is quite fantastic. And by now it probably is.

All the lonely people

I saw Leigh Bowery on stage singing *Eleanor Rigby* once, in 1994, in a pub in Hoxton, in the East End. Lucian Freud was there at the bar drinking with Sarah Lucas. That seemed right, whereas in the past it would be hard to imagine their worlds colliding. But now it seems all the same world, Bohemia and Britpop. Francis Bacon would certainly be going round with Damien Hirst and the guitarist from Blur now, if Francis Bacon wasn't dead, and if Blur weren't out.

More stars

The other stars as great as Francis Bacon are Gilbert & George. There was a moment in the early 80s when there was an effort on the part of the artworld to dislike them on left-wing grounds, but this was soon given up.

Star rules

Francis Bacon, Gilbert & George, Damien Hirst. The biggest stars. Francis Bacon, although always a top star, stopped being a really fantastically good artist after a few years. Damien Hirst doesn't really do anything all that good any more in art, unless he's quickly done something while this book is at the printers. But that doesn't matter according to the star rules, and in any case he might still do great advertising or films, even though nobody much liked his Blur video or his film with Keith Allen.

Shit and Cunt

Of them all only Gilbert & George stayed true to their made-up selves. One of their first works was a photo of their youthful art school selves holding up handwritten signs, or maybe they were sewn on their jumpers, saying Gilbert the Shit and George the Cunt. They said they were living sculptures, and they were.

Ever since they started, people would ask if they really were like the way they behaved publicly. Their funny, stiff, uptight manner and stiff suits. Didn't they drop the act in private, or when they were among

friends? But they never do drop the act, although that doesn't mean it isn't an act, and they really are sincere artists, although it's hard to know why that's good. I mean they really are good but it's hard to explain how being sincere and totally made-up at the same time can work, and why that should result in excellence.

Their attackers always overdo it and call them evil and fascist. But their defenders overdo it too and take Gilbert & George's slogans, which are always a bit absurd, like Art for All, and the things they say in interviews, which are also marvellously giddy, like We have developed a language which takes into account Man's inner self, at face value. As if they really are Messiahs.

Francis Bacon clichés

At 8.30 in the morning, I saw Francis Bacon on the escalator at South Kensington underground. Our top artist. We rarely think about his works critically. He was good at first, but then only did illustrational versions of his early inspired paintings. But he was always a magnificent star with a good act.

Perhaps he was on his way to the studio after a night of gambling and drinking champagne. As we know, the studio is small, at the top of a narrow staircase in a quiet South Kensington mews, with a single bare light bulb and a skylight, and a writhing masterpiece on the old-style wind-up easel. There is a chaos of brushes and paint cans and old newspapers and tubes of the most expensive purple and cadmium orange. There are trays of crumbly pastels, and sheets of Letraset, and bottles of fabric dyes. And books open at colour reproductions of infected mouths, and paintings by Velazquez. The walls and door and mirror have all been used as a palette.

Francis Bacon *Head VI* 1949

As he glides up the moving stairs, the station begins to hum with Francis Bacon clichés. Art after Auschwitz hums first. The horrors of the twentieth century. Totalitarianism and the Bomb. The human condition

Francis Bacon *Lying Figure* 1969

theme. We are just sides of meat. The theatre of cruelty. Expression shooting out of nerve endings in the finger-tips. Blobs of flung white. Not bourgeois decoration. Life summed up by a dog turd he saw in the gutter once. Painting at night by the bare light bulb on inspiration and champagne. Blurred hallucination realism. Erotic male flesh. Velazquez. Muriel Belcher. John Deakin. Who were they, anyway? The nanny's broken glasses from *Battleship Potemkin*. Fivers and ten-bob notes. Bottles and glasses and toilets and sinks and sick. Soho. Fitzrovia. Mayfair. Wheeler's and the Colony Room. Matisse backgrounds. Going to Tangiers. Not standing for any small talk. Drinking with criminals and aristocrats. Not cleaning your brushes except on the curtains of the Savoy. Screaming Popes in Adolph Eichmann war crimes trial cages. Paraplegic children on all fours photographed by Muybridge. Not going to the museum in Rome when in Rome but doing screaming male flesh purple power Popes from photos instead. Having museum glass over your paintings, and gold frames, and doing triptychs when one would do, and charging a million pounds.

He fades away into Old Brompton Road and the fabulous hum dies down. Laughing and gambling and wearing make-up.

John Stezaker

One of the well known Conceptual artists of the London artworld of the 70s was John Stezaker. Others were Victor Burgin, Art & Language, who were a group and actually lived near Oxford rather than in London, and John Hilliard. There were others, of course, but I can't remember them now. They've all faded out of the limelight, like John Stezaker has. Although, like him, they sometimes fade back in again briefly. I only remember these ones because I've met some of them. John Stezaker always used to do movie stills, or pictures from magazines, with something slightly changed. Like the head of a figure from a nudist magazine being cropped. Which was a bit offensive, of course, and he probably wishes he hadn't done that now.

Everyone did a lot of photo-montages in the 70s. In series. There was one I remember seeing, featuring a TV screen with the shoes of the TV viewer shown in the frame, as if the montage was a photo taken of the TV screen by the TV viewer. The shoes were working boots, so there was an idea about class.

Artists often made points about class, in defiance of formalism which only made points about form. But now class issues are very rarely the issue in art. Just as formalism is rarely an issue.

But John Stezaker's montages were usually just about dreams or uncanny sights. The pictures he faded back in again with in the 80s, were actually more 60s in feel. Not so much of 60s artworld art, but 60s graphics, from underground magazines like *International Times* or *Oz*. There was a style at that time that was a re-run of Max Ernst-type montages, which I see in my mind's eye, remembering back to when I used to read those things in early teenage, as engravings of sexy women and machinery mixed up in photo-collage dreamscapes. For some reason this style keeps returning. And this is the style of his new big photo-montages, which the young artists who run the gallery at Cubitt Street Studios, behind King's Cross, invited him to show there the other day. They looked intense and kinky, men merged with women in a strange way. And trees that looked human. That's a psycho science fiction look which is strong in popular culture now, but he was interested in it at an early stage. I first met him in 1981 and he said his favourite type of image was the clean open large-scale hard-edge abstract art of the 60s, and I thought that was good, because you'd probably think he would have said Marcel Duchamp. I can't think of anyone who is really obsessed about Duchamp any more, except conservative critics who want to blame him for everything.

Quivering

In the ads section of *Flash Art* this month there was a full-page open letter by the artist brothers Jake and Dinos Chapman, which was addressed to Martin Maloney, a recent arrival in the pages of *Flash Art*. He had written sarcastically about the brothers' sculptures and their personalities, in the previous issue. Even though an example of their extremely shocking and outrageous work was on the front cover. A realistic child with an erect penis instead of a nose, or a still from their video of two porn actresses having sex with a dismembered head with an erect penis nose. Or something in that general area that the Chapmans have made so uniquely their own.

Their letter ranted and raved with bitter humour. It wound up with a story that might have been true or a joke, about how the brothers had pretended to cry down the phone to the critic's answering machine, and Martin Maloney had picked up the receiver in mid-cry and, with a quivering voice, said that at least their work had been on the front cover.

The Legend of Jake

According to legend, Jake Chapman was once in a terrible fight after an artworld event one evening, that resulted in his hospitilization. And

Jake Chapman

then when he got out, all covered in plaster and on crutches, somehow the fight started up again, even though his limbs were already all broken. I only know this legend in its roughest outline, but naturally I passed it on years later, when the Chapmans were famous, to a journalist who had phoned to ask what I knew about their work. I never thought about it again until I activated my own answering machine one morning and got an earful of sputtering fucks and fucking hells and cunts from Jake, in response to the article that had resulted from this journalist's phone call. I was shaken and promptly called the Chapmans' gallery to find out Jake's phone number, which I'd lost, since I wasn't particularly in the habit of phoning him, since actually I hardly know him. Even though I'm calling him Jake now. Although I did once do some filming in his studio and have lunch with him and Dinos.

And, yes, they were extremely enjoyable company. They told a very good story about how they'd been menaced on the motorway in Holland by a carful of Malaysian drug-dealer psycho thugs, and how they and their friend all thought they were going to die. They called the police from a service station but the police wouldn't come. Then their friend went into a dreadful fear fit, like in *The Deerhunter* when the American captives are having to shoot themselves in the heads, and howled to

Jake and Dinos Chapman's studio

the police on the phone that they were all going to die and wait till his father heard about it. The brothers began to hate their friend and be afraid of him and they all went through terrible personality crack-ups. But they escaped in the end.

So I got his number from Victoria Miro, the gallery that shows them, and dialled it, and the answering machine answered and I claimed in an honestly quivering voice that I really didn't know this journalist and I'd hardly even mentioned this obviously irrelevant and unimportant and in any case quite personal hospitalization story to the journalist.

Which was more or less true. Or less really, since although I didn't know the journalist I had relished telling the story and really emphasized it because it seemed very good and I couldn't think of anything informative or wise to say about the Chapmans' work, as it seemed to speak for itself.

Jake and Dinos Chapman

The Chapmans' work

Their first really effective shocking work was a table-top model of every one of Goya's *Disasters of War* etchings, perfectly realized in 3D form using Airfix model soldiers that had been mutilated and distorted with penknives and then carefully painted. The Airfix model soldiers were all now late eighteenth-century Spanish monks and civilians and inquisitors and soldiers and rebels, realistically castrating and burning and burying each other alive on a perfect white table top.

Then they took one of the tableaux, *Great Deeds Against the Dead*, where Goya shows mutilated naked body parts hung on a tree, and they realized that, in horribly life-size 3D form, using shop-window mannequins and wigs and a life-size fibreglass model tree.

About the same time as this they were making realistic lifesize childen with sexual organs on their faces, gruesome vaginas or erections, and siamese-twin children with vaginas growing out of the join between the faces, and the Chapman parents covered with sexual organs and horrible gouged holes, like torture marks.

Then later on they made a life-size model of the physicist Steven Hawking on a mountain crag with real steam puffing out, called *Ubermann*, which was pretty cruel too. But before they did that, they made a table-top tableau of a brain and a penis, with a mechanical hammer hammering the brain and, with each blow, a spurt of semen-like white liquid ejaculating from the plastic penis.

Their trick, which so far has been completely effective, is to make all this seem very tied to real problems of modern life. But their *Flash Art* assailant, Martin Maloney, said it was just cynical sensationalism and only about making money and being stuck in an 80s mentality, and not at all in tune with the issues of the 90s. In another article he says the 90s are about flexibility and flow and being relaxed.

Jake and Dinos Chapman
The Disasters of War (detail) 1993

Art Monthly

Art Monthly is one of the oldest surviving British art magazines. For a long time there were always articles in it that were about what art should be. And then suddenly all that changed and there were only articles about Young British art. The ones about the purpose of art were always lumbering and slightly tedious in a way that was unique to *Art Monthly*. Whereas the Young British art ones are the same as all art magazine articles. Slick and clever and up-to-date. Thank God for Young British art!

The old stagers

Lucian Freud and **Francis Bacon** in Bacon's studio

R.B. Kitaj and The School of London

R.B. Kitaj *The Ohio Gang* 1965

The history of the American expatriate painter R.B. Kitaj includes his invention in 1976 of a school of painting which he called The School of London. He invented it for an exhibition called 'The Human Clay' which he curated for the Hayward Gallery. The school was him plus well known figurative painters like Frank Auerbach, Leon Kossoff, Lucian Freud, Francis Bacon, David Hockney. The idea was that figurative painting had not been killed by all the weird movements of Modernism but had just gone underground. And now that Modernism was faltering and going mad and was no longer believable, this underground art would surface and be recognized by the big institutions.

The School of London idea completely took off and was a big success, so now everybody knows what it stands for and there's no problem. Although on the whole we don't mention it much because it really is quite conservative and it's not all that interesting to think about. Just oldsters doing their charcoal life drawings and stuff.

Kitaj has been a London artist since the 60s. In those days he was a star associated with Pop Art, though not strictly himself a Pop artist. His paintings were hard-edged, bright-coloured and visually witty. He would just arbitrarily paint a line with masking tape across a graphically drawn figure, Rosa Luxembourg, say, or James Joyce, and it would look really good.

The main difference between his art and real Pop Art was that his was based on a wide range of high-minded literary subjects instead of a narrow range of everyday Pop culture subjects. But he soon moved much further away from Pop. In the 70s, when the Pop artists didn't know what to do, he started doing the old-fashioned charcoal drawing art, trying to make his art look more like Art, and initially including lots of virtually pornographic drawings of female nudes, which he later dropped when everyone was disgusted. Then he started up his new rough big brush-mark painting style that got more and more loose and fauvist, but was still very graphically reigned in, compared to the all-out

R.B. Kitaj

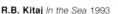

R.B. Kitaj *In the Sea* 1993

tortured expressionism of some of the other School of London painters such as Frank Auerbach or Leon Kossoff. But with much more heightened, bright, acidic colours than theirs.

And that's where he is now. He is a big seller and has works in the Saatchi collection. But recently he has been attacked a lot. He had a retrospective at the Tate Gallery that the critics cruelly shot down. There was too much information on the labels, it was said. He explained too much and was pompous and couldn't even draw. But what is drawing anyway? It's like formalism, no one knows what it is any more.

Kitaj often does bits and pieces of writing, and one of the hallmarks of his writing style is the seemingly offhand but obviously quite loaded, for him, asides about how he thinks he is perceived by his critics. That is, too fragmented, too difficult, too wordy, too impure. Which of course would all be quite good things to be, from a certain point of view. Whereas in reality the criticism all more or less homes in nowadays on the problem of him being too narcissistic and vain. Which he never seems to notice. But this is a human weakness we should be able to live with.

It's good the way he rambles on in his book *First Diasporist Manifesto*, about his own Jewishness and Jewishness generally and art and the twentieth century and the holocaust and Isaac Babel, and how they all connect.

Berlin

Another old stager is David Hockney, whose painting *Berlin*, from the 60s, is always appearing in stock shows at Waddington's. A stock show is a show of stock, rather than a real show. There's no real reason to see the art, other than that it's still in the gallery stock cupboards or storerooms or wherever they keep it. Because they haven't been able to sell it yet. Apparently Waddington can never sell *Berlin*, crisp and elegant and electric though it is. Or else he's always selling it and it's always coming back again.

David Hockney
Berlin: A Souvenir 1962

It has all the wit and talent and expressive use of different languages of representation, and sense of space and sophisticated colour and campery and cheek, and so on, that David Hockney was supposed to have had in the 60s, and really did have then.

He has become a strange old loony figure. Deaf and alone – except for sycophants, apparently, and his dog – and living in Los Angeles. Doing opera sets. And re-doing Picasso and Cubism and Matisse in a way that seems superfluous. There's still some electricity but he seems lost out there. He doesn't want to live in London because of the pettiness, he says.

In the early 80s there was a dismissive review by David Salle, one of the superstars of the New York artworld then, in *Artforum* about him, where he said Hockney was just completely irrelevant to anything, and he couldn't understand why anyone paid any attention to him. At times you can almost agree with that kind of attitude, because obviously Hockney is such a sacred cow. But at least his character goes on changing and developing in an interesting way.

Lucian Freud

The grandson of Sigmund Freud, he is the pet of the older art critics. They love his myth and always retell it when they're writing about him, as if it hadn't been heard a million times before. There's something stuck and boring about the world of Freud, that you instinctively want to reject, without analysing your prejudice.

Not his world exactly – after all, how much do we really know of it? More the cult of him. You reject the kind of people who go on about him, and it's always a bit surprising when somebody you thought you knew turns out to be a Freud cult member. At the same time his paintings are compelling in a way. He paints as if even Cézanne never existed, let alone Marcel Duchamp. But his paintings are quite intense.

Or are they? I don't even know for sure. He's one of those mythic artists where the myth is so strong it's hard to tell what's going on. Like the only survivor of Abstract Expressionism, Willem de Kooning. Except de Kooning is obviously quite good, because of all the painterly energy of his Women series of the 50s, when he was a kind of Abstract Expressionist sex fiend, and the way those women have blue heads and yellow bodies. And the way in the 60s he just went very loopy and drunk and on tranquillisers, and the colour was all high and wild and feminine, and the figures became outrageously cartoony and lazy and just slid down the canvas as if he didn't care what you thought, and was painting for Rubens not for you.

Lucian Freud *Benefits Supervisor Resting* 1994

Lucian Freud certainly is boring as far as colour is concerned, he just does brown. But he goes on stalking the model and painting it like a surgeon and dissecting it and really looking, and all the other

Lucian Freud
Reflection (Self-portrait) 1985

mythic things he's supposed to do in his studio. So you have to hand it to him in the end. He really is a star.

The main points of his myth are that he always drove everywhere in a Rolls Royce but maintained the same old run-down studio in Paddington. He had lots of women, who were all aristocrats. And when one was used up he just got another one and he had different children by them all, who all grew up to be novelists and TV presenters.

In one rare interview, he said he never spoke to his brother Clement Freud who used to do Chum commercials. Obviously we respect him for that. And although he probably could do with some therapy, he was sceptical about the discoveries of his grandfather and he said life was too short for psychoanalysis.

He came over from Berlin in the War and he started painting as a teenager. He always painted in a flat enamel obsessively detailed style and was famous for that. He did a very tender portrait of Francis Bacon in that style in the 50s, but it was stolen from the National Gallery in Berlin a few years ago. And then in the 60s he started painting more loosely with big brushes, gradually focusing in on the image instead of flatly spelling it out inch by inch across the canvas with tiny brushes. And some of his former champions dropped him because of that, but he didn't care.

And now he does these very crusty brown paintings of figure groups or single figures or heads, with dramatic croppings, so at least he paints as if Degas existed. And the scenes are all made up of thick crusty paint but are very realistic at the same time. So to some extent the naked bodies seem to come together in the eye as bodies from a distance. And then partly break up into crusts close to. But the main aspect of the paintings is the realistic bleak stark nakedness of the figures, and the invitation to stare, which is creepy and disturbing, and you have to wonder about those older critics.

His myth overlaps a lot with Francis Bacon's. They used to drink champagne together and go around laughing in their taxis and Rollses, gambling all night in Mayfair and losing huge sums because they were Existential, and their defenders really loved that. Whereas it seems a bit of a drag to us nowadays, because we're more spiritual. But then they fell out in the 70s and never made up. Some of Francis Bacon's best portraits are of Freud. They always look like him, even though they're distorted. But Freud only did that one portrait of Bacon and it's a marvel of magic realism. Not really realistic, but not distorted either. And now it's hanging in a burglar's apartment somewhere.

Always dark

Gilbert & George *George the Cunt Gilbert the Shit* 1970

Sculpture

There isn't a line of painting, with a clear progression of dominant styles, in London art, as there has been in New York art, which you can trace from the post-war period to now. But there is one of sculpture. At least up to the early 80s. After that it gets a bit more confusing.

Lynn Chadwick
Boy and Girl 1959

At first it was big rounded forms expressing nature and man's feminine side by Henry Moore. This was a kind of provincial Modernism influenced by Picasso. After the war it was Geometry of Fear sculpture, which was theatrical angular expressionist sculptures of suffering man by Lynn Chadwick and Reg Butler. This must have been really bad because no one remembers it at all now.

Then there was abstract sculpture by Anthony Caro which started in the early 60s after Caro had been been Henry Moore's assistant. He was doing ordinary clay and plaster sculptures of figures for a few years but then he went to America and saw some abstract paintings of stripes and targets and met the New York critic Clement Greenberg, and all these factors made him start welding steel shapes together to make abstract forms, and getting his wife to paint them with gloss paint so they seemed strangely weightless. This was Late Modernism.

Anthony Caro *Capital* 1960

About the same time, there was a big wave of funny-shaped wacky looking sculptures called things like *Tra La La* – which was a real sculpture by Philip King – and painted in very unserious colours, which was influenced by the Pop mood of the 60s while still remaining completely abstract. This was called New Generation scupture. Everyone liked it, but it only lasted a few years. It was still Modernism but not as important as Caro.

Then it was back over to Anthony Caro again, and there was a hegemony of everyone doing welded steel abstract sculptures like his, for a long time, and then it was mockingly called the heavy metal style. It was Late Modernism still

Philip King *Twilight* 1963

lingering on, when Modernism had ended. And at last there was a revolt against it, with artists just going for walks and calling it a sculpture or singing *Underneath the Arches* and calling that a sculpture too. This was Late Modernism but also Post-Modernism, confusingly overlapping. Then there was another wave of the wacky stuff in the early 80s, which was called New Object Sculpture, and that was Post-Modernism.

And that was really the end of the line of big sculpture movements, because the next big movement was Young British art which obviously isn't primarily a sculpture movement, although there are some sculptors in it. Like Rachel Whiteread who does casts of things. A room, a house, a bed. And Damien Hirst who does vitrines, but also paintings. And Sarah Lucas, who does casts of her armpits. And the Chapman brothers who do sex sculptures.

Young British art is really a movement of everything mixed up and everyone chopping and changing between different mediums and styles and nobody ever particularly mentioning the word sculpture, even as a weird kind of arch joke, which was the way Gilbert & George used to mention it when they said their photographs were sculptures.

Gilbert & George *The Singing Sculpture* 1970

Heavy metal

In the 60s there was another art school that was fashionable, as well as the Royal College of Art – where Pop Art started – and that was Saint Martin's in Charing Cross Road. There were fashion and film departments there, but the main style in the art department was what became known as heavy metal sculpture. This style has so disappeared now that it's hard to remember it ever existed. It was abstract shapes of metal, twisting and turning.

It was called heavy metal in the 70s, when it was still lingering on, as an insult. By then everyone could see its time was up. Now in the 90s it's as if it simply never existed, because we think of the 60s as Andy Warhol or David Hockney or Bridget Riley, whose art was clearly tied into popular culture. Whereas heavy metal acted as if popular culture never existed. It was a war between heavy metal and popular culture, and we know who won.

In the 60s abstract metal sculpture was the international avant-garde sculpture style, but the conservative side of the avant-garde. The opposite side was fashionable and fun. The heavy metal side was pipe-smoking and solemn. It was ruled by Anthony Caro, who is now a knight. He still does the style and probably sells his stuff OK too. But we can't really see it. There's no category for it any more, it doesn't mean anything, we just don't register it.

At Saint Martin's, under Anthony Caro's regime, the students and teachers there, in the sculpture department, used to do these heavy metal sculptures using old or new bits of metal and welding gear. They would do their welding and then they would all stand around the sculptures and criticize them and smoke their roll-ups and pipes and then go away and make better ones. No one knew why really. It was the equivalent of figurative artists in the 70s going on doing figuration against all the odds, as if figuration itself, rather than what was being represented, or any other quality or aspect that the figurative work might have, was a virtue, its own reward.

The rebels against heavy metal at Saint Martin's in the late 60s were Barry Flanagan, Bruce McLean, Gilbert & George and Richard Long. Anthony Caro's creed was that sculpture didn't have to be marble or clay, it could be made out of anything, which of course, as the creed set in, was understood as, 'as long as it's welded metal'. The point about the rebels was that for them anything could be sculpture really and truly, which in a way was a credo powerfully influenced by Caro, although the acknowledged influence would not have been Caro but Joseph Beuys, who said that everyone is an artist.

Barry Flannagan
Light on light on sacks 1969

Everything is a sculpture

Everything the rebels did they called sculpture, in a serious way, although it was a kind of joke as well. With the exception of Barry Flanagan, they didn't really do objects any more. They did actions and photographs. Barry Flanagan still did objects but they were only hessian sacks or rays of light. The rebels were all quite funny, except Richard Long who was serious.

Gilbert & George were funny in a different way from Bruce McLean. Bruce McLean did more or less outright comedy art, in performance form, which at first really was quite amusing, like his imitations of modern art sculptures, where he would have himself photographed lying on a white plinth posing as a sculpture by Henry Moore or Anthony Caro. But then after a while he did comedy art in painting or sculpture form, with happy, bright colours and jolly forms. And then gradually he just did a kind of standard decorative vaguely Matisse-influenced modern art painting and sculpture, not particularly funny at all, as if he wanted to show he wasn't afraid of ordinary loveliness.

But Gilbert & George were always a bit dark. They're the only art act that can do that robotic besuited behaviour that they do and not be embarrassing. As we know, the style has been taken on by many others from all different tribes. Music, fashion, film, art, whatever. It was really big in the early 80s. Somehow with the others you want to give them a good shaking and make them join the army. But with Gilbert & George the robotic act works excellently.

Those first Saint Martin's rebels have all developed in their various ways, though they all have the comfortable aura of those who have been constant stars. Gilbert & George, the most starry, do their stained glass window-type huge photograph pictures, which are always shocking and massively attended to and looked at and talked about, and they have penises and turds and flowers and urban landscapes in them.

By coincidence, I happened to be in their studio only this morning and they were showing off some good photos of new works that were about

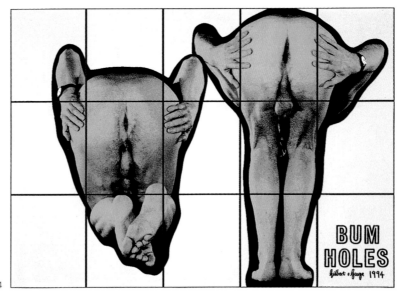

Gilbert & George *Bum Holes* 1994

to be exhibited in New York and France. Hugely enlarged microcosmic images of sperm and blood and faeces, and their own naked selves bending down and showing their anuses, called things like *Bum Holes* and *Bloody Shit House*.

I'll be in New York when you're show is on, I said, and George said, Good, come to the spunk party. Then they said they'd bought the empty house next door to theirs in Fournier Street, and when I asked what they were going to do with it, Gilbert said, Make it into a bordello. And George said, A children's bordello.

But nobody particularly thinks about the other rebels any more. Richard Long used to go for a walk and it was a sculpture, or put some stones on the floor and that would be a sculpture too, or pour some water down a mountain. But now he does a much more frankly decorative art of stone arranging or pattery mud paintings on the wall with artful drips.

Saint Martin's painting

Saint Martin's as a legendary place started grinding to a halt in the 80s and finally petered out altogether at the end of the decade when it became part of The London Institute and just like any other art school.

There had been a style of painting as well as one of sculpture associated with it, which grew up in the 70s and lasted a long time. It didn't disappear as dramatically as heavy metal sculpture for some reason, maybe because it was by nature more loose and open and adaptable and eclectic. Also it didn't have a name. Also it wasn't only associated with St Martin's, but was in all the art schools and all the studios everywhere. It was vague by nature. But like Saint Martin's sculpture, it was one of those things that was really definitely there and in everyone's consciousness for a while, and then suddenly was vaporized and nobody is quite sure why. As if it was flying saucers that did it in, or an HIV of painting.

Gilbert & George *Bloody Shit House* 1997

There isn't anything to say about it really, it was pretty harmless and I certainly don't wish it any harm. You did it with great big pots of acrylic that were ordered on Fridays in Valerie's, the cake shop on Old Compton Street, from a man who ran a paint company called Spectrum. You would take all these pots of paint back to the studio in Wapping where all the studios were and whack loads of the stuff over big areas of cotton duck. And if it was the 60s or 70s you would call it *Untitled*. Or if it was the 80s, and you were still doing it, you would call it something wine bar-y or Eric Clapton-y, like *Smooth Lady* or *Foxy Tequila*. You were probably teaching somewhere, three days a week, and not exhibiting much any more and generally leading a quiet life.

Mad, dreadful

The Turner Prize

The Turner Prize, the artworld's Britpop awards, started in 1984. Now it feels like it was always there. At least nobody cares much any more about where it came from. Each year it gets more and more established and believable. And the exhibitions of the nominated artists' works get more and more formidable, like real museum shows. It's not fundamentally evil. Anybody could walk into it and get something from the art, as they could from any exhibition, but even more so now that the works get so much breathing room.

But at the same time, because of what it is, a flim-flam media event, it presents a strange cartoon image of what actually goes on in art. The press announcements, the TV programmes, the interviews and articles, the speeches and ceremonies, all build up into an artwork on its own, with its own mad, dreadful meaning, that confusingly overlaps with the mad or silly meanings of the artworks on show.

This invisible artwork, of gassy hype, is ghastly and solemn. All the good things about art, anything chancy or normal or human or casual or inspired, are vacuumed out, with only sad plodding pretentious undead zombie nonsense allowed to remain. The bad things. Everyone involved must sense something is wrong, but nobody can think how to do it any other way. Everyone plays along, the artists as much as anyone else. It's just the realism of the situation.

The Turner Prize is crying out for a Jarvis Cocker-style stage assault. Jarvis Cocker, the singer in Pulp, jumped onstage and larked about during a Michael Jackson performance at the 1996 Brit Awards, a musical event, making everyone laugh and gasp and suddenly realize they didn't have to go along with the phoniness and emptiness of this – or perhaps any – corporate ceremony. It was one of the important cultural moments of the year.

But strangely, the actual assaults on the Turner Prize, the K Foundation's famous anti-Turner Prize event, for example, in 1994, miss the target somehow. They're too credulous of the officialized discourse. They try and be the same, all Conceptual-arty and falsely avant-garde and clever, instead of trying to just normalize an excruciating event. Which was Jarvis Cocker's great achievement.

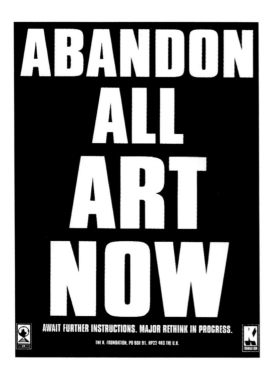

The K Foundation ad campaign 1994

But then the other day I had to change my mind about that because Jarvis Cocker was on a TV programme about the Turner Prize and he was as boring as everybody else.

Anyway, all the other things about the Turner Prize are good, or at least not the Turner Prize's fault. For example, the fact that it's always alienated Post-modern art that's nominated. It isn't the Turner Prize's fault that that's the main art now. The Turner Prize is too mad and inert and ridden by a vacuous, painful, snob attitide towards culture to take the credit for that whole problem.

The K Foundation

The K Foundation is made up of two people. One of them drew hobbit posters for Arena, the publishers, and made a lot of money from that. Before being the K Foundation they were KLF, a successful dance band of the 80s and early 90s. As KLF, they laughed and sneered at the pop music industry but made good records anyway, and they published a book on how to make a hit. They were fed up with the music world. They thought it was shallow. So they started putting on subversive art events instead. They mounted a campaign to subvert one of the Turner Prizes, offering £40,000, which was twice the amount of the real Prize money, to the worst artist instead of the best one. They gave it to Rachel Whiteread. She turned it down at first but then took the money and gave it out in bits to other artists.

Then the K Foundation burned a million pounds in real money, and because it was about the same time as their Turner Prize event it all seemed connected, something to do with money and hype and the public's credulity and the end of art.

Corporate boredom

The Tate Gallery shop. Is the shop the main reason for the Tate Gallery's existence? Is the purpose of art masterpieces to have jigsaws and diaries and headscarves made of them?

In some of the former Eastern bloc countries of Europe there are new museums of modern art opening up. They didn't have them under

Communism because modern art was considered decadent then, so you couldn't have a museum of it. Now they've all got these museums starting from scratch, or with a bit of a permanent collection from pre-1945 and some odds and ends from later decades picked up in a hurry since 1989.

Some of the directors of these new museums are really bright. I met one in Prague recently and he said he saw the Tate Gallery, like the Guggenheim Museum in New York, or the Museum of modern art there, as a model of how modern art museums in the West atrophied and died in the 80s and 90s because all the energy was directed at jigsaw puzzle and prize and sponsorship problems, and none at all at questioning how things are.

These new post-Communist museums will have to have all those extra things because the same realism now applies to them as to us, he said. But in starting from zero, with their new idealism and curiosity about the world, they'll be in a position to do something really different and better or something.

I don't know. I can't remember what the different thing was now. In fact thinking about it I'm sure he would have only had some rather dry seminar programme or other in mind. Or revisionist historical exhibitions that prove a Czech artist was doing Cubism before Picasso. And there would be jigsaw puzzles of Franz Kupka instead of Richard Serra.

Something's wrong

Angela Bulloch

'Something's Wrong' 1994 curated by Bob and Roberta Smith: work by Matthew Collings (photo/painting installation) and Bob and Roberta Smith

'Something's Wrong' 1994 curated by Bob and Roberta Smith: work by Bob and Roberta Smith

'Candyman II' 1994
curated by Peter Lewis and Matthew Arnatt
foreground Bob and Roberta Smith
background Matthew Collings

More warehouse shows

After 'Freeze' there were a few more warehouse shows before the warehouse phenomenon became an institution. But soon a flood of warehouse shows started, many of them actually in former warehouses, though sometimes not. But still more or less thought of as warehouse shows. The flood continues today. Everyone has been in at least one. The shows are in the north or south parts of east London, or in south London, or on the edge of the City, in the Old Street area.

From a certain perspective these shows are all inter-changeable. There's often no electricity so that if you arrive at all late you can't see anything. And the toilets are often not working or not installed at all. The spaces can be dangerous. Especially the dockland ones where the doors are often not secured, with the opening simply leading into empty space, and there is a strong likelihood of someone walking out of a warehouse show to their death.

The shows are usually a bit silly or giddy intellectually, with interchangeable titles and a lot of art objects that seem neither here nor there. The art is in a secret code. Everyone involved understands it. Nobody else does. That's it.

I am sometimes invited to be in these shows, I don't know why. Once I was in a warehouse show called 'Candyman II' (after a horror film by the same name, no other reason). It was held in a warehouse somewhere near Rotherhithe. It had been a biscuit warehouse or a biscuit factory or something and the building still smelled of fat or lard or biscuit mixture, and the walls were sticky in a slightly disgusting way.

A man phoned me up and asked if I would be in this show and I said Yes. I went to the building with some of the other artists. I didn't know any of them. We went round the huge, high ceilinged, thoroughly birdshat spaces. On this particular morning it was brightly sunlit, dirty, powerfully atmospheric, biscuit smelling. The man said the owner of the building

SOMETHING'S WRONG

REVIEWERS:

WRITE AN INSTANT REVIEW WITH OUR HELP!

SOMETHING'S WRONG is the ___ *WORST* _____ show I have

seen for quite some time. The work is particularly ___ *POOR* _____.

The show features: Matthew Collings, Justine Daff, Stephen Glynn, John Issacs,

Philip King, Hilary Lloyd, Brighid Lowe, Simon Morse, Victor Mount,

Janette Parris, Bob & Roberta Smith and Jessica Voorsanger.   I would like to

single out ___ *M. COLLINGS* ____ for special attention as he/she is

clearly ___ *TARGITED* ___. The building it is in is __ *WET* __

_____ and the artists are ___ *LAME* _____. I would

advise the public to _ *BRING A SPRAY CAN!*

Questionnaire from 'Something's Wrong' 1994

would be paying for the walls to be cleaned. Or painted if we wanted. And for lighting. And there would be a catalogue and a private view and an ad in *Art Monthly*.

Then we all went away and did our works. I did something I hoped was more or less in the code and after a few months we were all happy to see our ad in *Art Monthly* with our names correctly spelled. And then we all got vans and went to the building and installed our works. One work was an electric fence. There were some paintings done in biro. The private view went as normal. The bar was near the electric fence. Some people from Israel came round and some of the artists were invited to show there.

Another show I was in was held in a warehouse in Bermondsey Street and was called 'Something's Wrong'. On the opening night, pints of Thunderbird were served and there was a man cleaning shoes as an artwork. You have to be pretty tough to be in these shows.

Private views

Private views are emotionally quite intense, although the emotions are never expressed, they just go on in your head. On the outside you appear normal and go around saying Hi! brightly, or, Hmm, that's interesting. But inside you are reeling. The shocks come fast and hard. Regular private view goers all have disintegrated personalities and are suffering from post-traumatic stress syndrome.

Euro

I go to Warren Street to the opening of a new gallery there with a name that is either Richard Pryor, the American comedian who set fire to himself, or Robert Quine, the balding guitarist on Lou Reed's late 80s solo albums.

It turns out Robert Prime is a made up name and the gallery is really run by an Italian or Belgian man and that's maybe why the atmosphere of the gallery, with its bright, white, good design, and bits of brightly coloured knick-knack artworks dotted about – glimpsed through the crowds of people, made of photos and felt pen drawing and glass and masking tape, all of it reasonable according to late 90s art laws – is more of a Milan or Brussels atmosphere than a strictly London one. A group show of Euro and London young art. Young London art is the main thing in international art so it's only natural that new Euro galleries are opening here now instead of in Europe.

India

Upstairs the art is all one show by Dominique Gonzales-Foerster, who is French I think, of photos of anything, including one lot of photos of a Le Corbusier state housing complex in India. These photos are in books and displayed behind coloured plexiglass sheets. The housing design is typically Le Corbusier but with Indian design creeping over the Corbusier look.

Cooling towers

Downstairs where the group show is, it's more crowded with people as the bar and food are down there too. At the bottom of the stairs where it's most congested, there's one colour photo of an interior of some kind, a restaurant or a train station or a museum, by Candida Höfer, the German artist who was taught by Bernd and Hilla Becher, the 60s German couple who take photos of cooling towers. There are other bits and pieces, but no centre. There are some felt pen drawings behind glass with the framing coming apart more and more as the evening goes on.

Chinese

Further into the crowded space there's a work on a wall which is two overlapping sheets of strongly coloured fabric, orange and red perhaps, stuck down with pieces of beige tape. Beside the work is a computer print-out text by its creator Liam Gillick, which no one is reading. I see Angela Bulloch who looks odd. I'm just talking empty static and I say mindlessly, Oh that's a nice work by Liam I saw. But I don't know until a bit later on that her long-standing relationship with him has just ended due to him being in another relationship with an American artist who does paintings of words, which are now on show at Jay Jopling's gallery, White Cube. I learn all this within a few minutes from other people, but

Private view at Independent Art Space March 1997

in the meantime her face is going all dismayed and she says, Well I've got something here too. So this would have been a *faux pas* anyway even without the relationship complication, so I apologize and say I'm going to look for it straight away. And when I find it, it's a giant bean bag with a TV set showing a video of some Chinese girls sitting around. So later I see her again and I say, Did you film those Chinese girls yourself? And she says they're Japanese girls and she was in Japan for three months.

The Italian or Belgian guy who maybe runs the gallery and who is a writer for *Flash Art*, is introduced to me. I recognise him from the Venice Biennale. He says he has the tape of a short film I made about there, but I think he must be lying because I'm sure I didn't use his interview.

Bill Withers

Then I see Angus Fairhurst, who once redirected all the main West End galleries' phone lines as an artwork, so when the directors or their assistants phoned someone up they got through to the assisant or director of another gallery instead and they couldn't understand what was happening. I tell him someone was praising him to me the other day and saying he was the artworld's secret weapon. He says, What do you mean? And I say they said he is very clever and gives all the young London artists their ideas including Damien Hirst.

But I'm only being light and in the parenthesis in my head I'm thinking, This is untrue, or very simplifying. And actually our talk was more about our amazement at the conversation style of the young London artists, when you first meet one, which is unbelievably inane usually. Although we don't think their work is that. I mean it's not like we're so deep. We're just amazed they can get away with that way of talking when everyone else in life has to make an effort or they'd soon be shunned socially. But anyway Angus Fairhurst says, How do you make a duck soulful? I don't know the answer. He says, You put it in the oven until its bill withers.

The drink is red and white wine, mineral water and chilled Rolling Rock, and the food is a huge hunk of fresh parmesan on a plate with a knife, so you can just hack bits off. A new private view idea.

Angus Fairhurst

Martin McGeowan director of Cabinet Gallery (left) and **Jeremy Deller**

Then suddenly these red and white wine and Rolling Rock drunks are in an Indian restaurant in another street and my conversation is staying on its completely wrong course, as I say to Samantha Taylor Wood, who once exhibited a photo of herself with love bites on her neck, called *Slut*, and another one of herself in a T-shirt with the printed slogan Suck Fuck Spank Wank, and has made a number of films, including one of herself dancing to a soundtrack of machine gun fire, that the only reason she wants to eat these free curries is that she's jealous she's not in this show and there's really no reason to eat at all at this time of night. And I give my plate to Andrew Wheatley. Perhaps he's related to Dennis Wheatley, the famous author of *The Devil Rides Out*. Andrew Wheatley is one of the directors of the Cabinet Gallery in Brixton, which certainly has a Satanic atmosphere. And that's where you can currently see the work of Jeremy Deller, who does art about pop culture, even though he studied Italian baroque painting at the Courtauld Institute, and who's here now in his 90s youth fashion clothes. Whereas Andrew Wheatley always wears 80s suits. And soon I'm eating rolled up nan breads one after the other.

Individuals

Individuals. This is what the art scene is made up of. Luckily, because of fear of loneliness, many of them run around in packs, otherwise it would be impossible to generalize or simplify ruthlessly what it is they do. The really awkward to simplify individuals are artists like Rose Finn Kelcey who isn't in a pack as far as I know. Although she is a very good artist, what does she do that you can neatly sum up? A fridge at the Saatchi Gallery. A thing that had steam coming out of it at the

Rose Finn-Kelcey *Bureau de Change* 1988

Chisenhale Gallery. A picture of van Gogh's sunflowers made of coins at Robin Klassnick's Matt's Gallery, ten years ago, when it was in Hackney. The fridge and the steam sculpture are sensual whereas the coin thing is a comment on the art market. Maybe the van Gogh was just a mistake. Good job it was a long time ago. But also she did a lot of performances much longer ago in the 70s that I don't know anything about. Was she like Bobby Baker who used to do cookery as art? I don't know anything about her either. Or Sylvia Ziranek, who used to do performances with Bruce McLean?

Another individual is Robin Klassnik. He used to be an artist. He did mail art, where you had to post something yellow to him and he would add it to all the other yellow things that had been posted to him and they would all be a mail art artwork. Then he did some other types of art and then he opened his gallery, Matt's Gallery, which was named after his dog, Matt E. Mulsion, and he said running the gallery was art.

And another one is Richard Wilson, who used to exhibit at Matt's Gallery.

Richard Wilson

Richard Wilson is a very good artist. His used sump-oil installation called *20:50*, which is on permanent display at the Saatchi Gallery is very good, anyone could get it, which is what is good about all his artworks. He just takes everyday things, like a caravan or a window or a billiard table in a room, and transforms them into something new. He cuts them up and turns them inside out.

He is quite short and can go nuts when drunk, as I know from personal experience, although we have never exchanged more than a few words.

Richard Wilson *20:50* 1987

I used to share a bathroom with him in Rotherhithe, which is funny because one of his installations at Matt's Gallery was called *She Came In Through The Bathroom Window*.

Richard Wilson
She Came In Through the Bathroom Window 1989

The place where we shared a bathroom was a house which was actually two Acme houses joined together. Acme is a company that provides subsidized housing and studios for artists. I was living with Richard's ex-girlfriend, Ingrid Kerma, who is tall and German, and Richard was living with Sylvia Ziranek, the performance artist. It was virtually the same house, and the really fraught area was the bathroom. We would hear Sylvia muttering and cursing at us and sending bad vibes through the door when we were in there.

Anyway, Richard would sometimes come home at night drunk and, if it was winter, he would start whacking into lumps of wood with an axe, for the fire. Whack! Whack! Incredibly loudly. So one night it woke us up again and on this night I leapt out of bed and ran into the bathroom and began banging on the door to their bit of the house, yelling for him to stop. This was a mistake. The noise stopped, but suddenly there was another noise, of rushing feet on the stairs. And the door flew open and there was Richard, drunk and yelling back at me. A far greater force, even though in reality he is far smaller than me. I was a coward and started quaking and using that quivering voice again, and modifying my rough tones that I had been using when banging on his door, changing them to quivering middle-class tones, in the hope that a working-class person would never hit a middle-class person, like a man shouldn't hit a woman, or someone wearing glasses. Actually I do wear glasses but this was the middle of the night and I didn't have them on. Then Stefan, the teenage son of Ingrid, came in, and at the same time Sylvia appeared, and Stefan was calming Richard down, and Sylvia was looming there in the background, and I was in Ingrid's dressing gown quivering and backing out of the door.

So after that I didn't meet him again until five years later when I was working at the BBC, and I was round at Matt's Gallery presenting a short TV item about Richard constructing his excellent window sculpture, which was a spatial conundrum. He didn't mention that fateful night and he was as nice as pie.

Helen Chadwick

Helen Chadwick was an artist from the 70s. She was never quite accepted by the hard-core artworld but somehow stayed on, producing lots of shows. She did a lot of photo-based object things that were about identity and the body and gender and stuff. Eventually her outsiderness wore off and she became an insider just by still being around and doing the same thing.

But then she died suddenly in 1996 from a mysterious virus called myocarditus, which causes inflammation of the heart. It could have entered her body any time, years or hours before she died. But until

Helen Chadwick *Vanity* 1984

this was revealed by the coroner at the inquest, it was assumed she died of a heart attack and everyone was surprised because she always seemed healthy and didn't smoke. But actually the life of a medium successful artist who doesn't do straight sculptures or paintings – which can be shipped to shows, and then the artist just follows afterwards for the private view and a few days hanging around – is incredibly high on stress. If you do odd things that have to be installed idiosyncratically but very carefully, there's immense stress involved. You have to battle with officials and so on.

Stress

It's the hanging around that's probably the worst, even if you do normal art. Even when you're looked after it's alienating, and a lot of the time you're not looked after. When you're not looked after you just go around with your thoughts rattling round in your head, at the mercy of everyday pop culture, which is merciless. And when you are looked after, it's quite a strain too, to be with someone you don't really know for so many hours, making small talk endlessly.

You're in a strange place, living in your head, which is full of doubts which all start to rise very quickly and then fester horribly. And you're always waking up too early with a head full of this awful stuff. The ones who make it into their fifties and sixties and are still living this life – the original Conceptual artists, for example – how crazy they must be. How exhausted. How numbed. How long will it go on like this? they must wonder. When will it stop?

Crossed lines

Jack Wendler, the publisher of *Art Monthly*, who is in his sixties, told me he went up to Helen Chadwick once and said to her that he had seen a photo of her from the 70s in an exhibition of Fluxus memorabilia at the Tate Gallery. And she asked, was he trying to date her? And he was surprised and couldn't understand what she meant. Actually I couldn't understand what he meant either when he told me this story, because I thought he meant date in the sense of placing her in history, whereas he meant date in the sense of asking her out, which of course he wasn't doing, which was why he was surprised. Then another time he introduced the respected American art writer Thomas McEvilley to her at a party and Thomas McEvilley was drunk and he really did try to date her, and Jack Wendler had to apologize to her the next day on Thomas McEvilley's behalf.

Fluxus

Fluxus was an excellent international art movement that started up in the 60s and lingered on into the 70s. Lots of people were in it, including Joseph Beuys. It was about subverting the mass media and liberating art by doing anti-art things, like making films of water going down a plughole.

It couldn't survive of course, but like everything else it has its retro moments, and more and more glossy catalogues keep coming out about it all the time. And there are more and more commemorative shows, especially because Yoko Ono used to be in it, and she keeps being willing to get her old stuff out again. Actually it's doing Fluxus a disservice to remember it at all.

Yoko Ono showed a little thing on a ceiling in the 60s that you had to climb up a ladder to see. In the thing was the word Yes. When John Lennon climbed up the ladder and read that, he was relieved and it put him in a good mood, because he was expecting it to say Fuck You or No. And that's how he got to know Yoko.

Another Fluxus artist was the New Yorker, Al Hansun, who it turns out was the grandfather of Beck, the singer, who had a hit over here in 1994 with the slacker anthem *Loser*, which went, I'm a loser, baby, so why don't you kill me?

Ironic goo

Jake and Dinos Chapman with work in progress

From Bohemia to Britpop

In the 50s there was a strong sense of the London artworld being made up chiefly of Bohemians. My father was a Bohemian. He lived with Elisabeth Frink who was a star Existentialist Bohemian sculptress at a young age and later became a Dame. But then she died of cancer. Her bronze sculpture of a man on a horse can still be seen on the pavement in Albemarle Street, at least until recently when I was looking out for it and there were some roadworks there instead. And then I realized it was Dover Street that it was on.

My father had been a pilot in the war. He was in a prison camp in Germany and when he came back he had to go into hospital and have a leukotomy, which is a partial lobotomy. Eventually he committed suicide. He had a job once working at the Helen Lessore Gallery, where they showed the dark earnest encrusted Bohemian paintings of the era, David Bomberg and so on. He was often the worse for wear from drink and would sometimes steal the young Frink's belongings from her flat, her record player and stuff, and sell them to buy more drinks. After three years she ended the relationship under pressure from her family, and my father soon met and married my mother. And Elisabeth Frink generously went to the wedding and played guitar or something.

Model Bohemians

The model Bohemian in those days was Francis Bacon. But even then his myth was so strong and so distinctive that it transcended mere bohemianism.

Perhaps a better model is John Minton, who committed suicide and who did romantic figurative paintings in a style that seems to owe nothing to any modern art movement whatsoever. Or Gully Jimson, a fictional character from the widely read novel of the 50s, *The Horse's Mouth*, which was made into a film with Alec Guinness playing the artist Gully Jimson, who painted wild, ugly, glaring, outrageously corny Expressionist paintings, which were supplied for the film by the real life Bohemian painter John Bratby, who sadly died

from left to right: **Timothy Berens**, **Lucian Freud**, **Francis Bacon**, **Frank Auerbach** and **Michael Andrews** at Wheeler's

Gerald Wilde

recently. Or Gerald Wilde, the real life Bohemian that the character of Gully Jimson was partly based on, who was much too extremely Bohemian to get it together to do paintings for a film, and who painted quite sympathetic wild ugly Expressionist works that still turn up from time to time, on their warped stretchers.

Mustard

Keith Vaughan was another artist from those days. He hated Bohemians and especially Gerald Wilde, who he thought was just drunk and dirty. He said carrying on like that was some kind of post-Freudian thing, thinking you could just do anything you liked and not have any discipline.

Keith Vaughan did quite nice post-Cézannian paintings that nobody remotely cares about any more, but which I quite like. He was fantastically kinky and he really was literally an amazing wanker. He had a special black box that he used to wind up and get orgasms from. He did his four hours of painting each morning standing at the easel working, with mustard under his foreskin or pins stuck in the end of his penis.

He was against the hippies in the 60s, of course, but he had a soft spot for Hells Angels, who he said were virile and heroic, and it was a great sadness of his life that he could never get to know any of them personally.

The Chelsea Arts Club

Unfortunately I imagine the London artworld's Bohemian period, which was the 1950s, as a ghastly time, mainly because the modern day survivors of it, or their imitators, who you come across at the Chelsea Arts Club, in Old Church Street, for example, seem so dreadful. Thank God for Britpop. Britpop artists are not primarily gruff angry men, and they don't scratch around with oil paints and corduroys, or drink in Finch's in the Fulham Road, or hang about the Colony Room in Soho hoping to catch sight of Francis Bacon and borrow five pounds off him.

The bridge between Bohemia and Britpop

The bridge between the awfulness of Bohemia in the 50s and the grooviness of Britpop in the 90s was Pop Art in the 60s, which according to legend started at the Royal College of Art in the late 50s.

At first Pop Art was a few paintings by Peter Blake of sweetshops and children wearing badges, and some quaintly futuristic exhibitions by Richard Hamilton and some architects, called things like *This Is Tomorrow*, with bubble cars and helicoptor diagrams and collages made of illustrations from *Science Now* and science fiction magazine covers.

Then it was David Hockney, Allen Jones, Derek Boshier, Peter Phillips, Joe Tilson and Gerald Laing, who all did paintings of tubes of toothpaste and Typhoo tea and watches and packaging and popular culture products mixed up with schematized renderings of the human figure, alienated modern man.

Bohemianism still survived in the London Pop Art of the 60s, as it perhaps didn't so much in New York Pop, I don't know. But at any rate as the 60s got going it was soon on the run. Berets and sword-sticks were definitely out. Actually sword-sticks are not so much Bohemian, more gentleman aristocrat, which is another strain of British art, that probably lingers on quietly somewhere outside London.

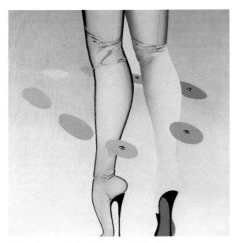

Allen Jones *Gallery Gasper* 1966–67

Pop Art clichés

Post-war Britain, austerity, black and white, rationing, the 50s, boredom. Suddenly Pop and consumerism, Michael Caine, California, swimming pools, packaging, Marshall McLuhan, working class, up north, polo neck, mini skirt, David Hockney receiving his Royal College of Art Diploma in a gold lamé suit and dyed hair because blondes have more fun.

Drive to Britpop

There was a swerve off the main course in the 70s, when London art went towards international Conceptual, Minimal, Performance Art and *Arte Povera*. *Arte Povera* means poor art and it refers to the materials used. The artists who did it originally in Italy would just do twigs and stuff, or maybe a herd of real horses eating straw in a gallery. That's the kind of thing that influenced Barry Flanagan to do hessian bags.

Then in the early 80s there was jokey Post-Modernist sculpture, which was thrown away household objects, collected up and arranged into a map of England, or cornucopias of plastic tomatoes, or washing machines turning into toy machine guns. This was called New Object Sculpture, to differentiate it from old object sculpture, which was welded metal abstract sculpture from St Martins. It was influenced by the attitude of the artists who rebelled against heavy metal by dematerializing the art-work, but it brought back material form again. That's why it was called New Object.

Also it was called Lisson Gallery sculpture because all the artists who did it showed at the Lisson Gallery and Nicholas Logsdail, who runs

the Lisson Gallery, was showing it there and in art fairs and international biennales. It never completely went away, unlike heavy metal, the style it replaced. But instead it just atrophied slightly into posh art by formerly young British artists now middle-aged and waiting for their knighthoods.

The seeds of the Britpop art of now were definitely there in New Object Sculpture and by the late 80s the real thing was at last underway. The Chelsea Arts Club and Finch's in Fulham Road, and even the Royal College of Art, just do not figure in this new Pop world, although, interestingly, Soho still does. In fact Britpoppers are no strangers to the Colony Room. They go there to ironically relive the myth of Francis Bacon.

Edward Allington
The Groan as a Wound Weeps 1984

Retro-Bohemian

And, weirdly, there is a strong streak of retro-Bohemianism running through the Britpop style. It is at its strongest – that is, hardest to tell where irony ends and full-on sincerism begins – in the Damien Hirst mythology, which is designed very much along Francis Bacon lines.

In this mythology Francis Bacon is considered the greatest artist. And the great corny subjects of Existentialist beatniks are considered genuinely worth mentioning. But in reality, as opposed to the myth, there is a strong sense about Damien Hirst's shock works of him testing the big Existentialist contents to see if they could be art (just as in his coloured spot paintings there is a sense of him testing spots to see if they could be painting) rather than actually expressing those contents. Seeing if life and death and sex and violence and alienation could work as art.

But perhaps that's always the way content makes its return in modern art. Perhaps it was the same for Picasso and Derain in the return to order period in the 1920s.

And perhaps it was the same for Francis Bacon himself. A lot of Francis Bacon is obviously short cuts to a received idea of deep content. But maybe he actually did hit some veins of the deep stuff, just by short-cutting across or around Cubism, or whatever other art baggage was holding back his Bohemian painter colleagues of the time.

Marc Quinn and the deep content

The deep content, with the high meaning, is always out there lurking. In the Groucho Club in Dean Street, which is three doors down from the Colony Room, you often see Marc Quinn, Damien Hirst's friend, who also does shocks. His first shock was his own head cast in eight pints of his own frozen blood (drawn over a period of time, so he didn't die) and presented in an Eichmann/Bacon glass box, standing on a science fiction refrigerator. In his recent works he gets more and more close to outright corniness, with his new Existentialist grey sculptures of an exploding body. As if he might be going back to the Bohemian period to see if there was anything they'd missed.

Marc Quinn
The Blind Leading the Blind 1995

Are shocks always the route to the deep content? When Jake and Dinos Chapman do their frightening forbidden fantasy sex subjects there's a definite surrounding ironic discourse goo that makes the work cool rather than just horrible. Even though, in our more sensitive moods, especially if we are parents, their works are actually rather horrible.

But when Marc Quinn does torn-up bodies and blood-heads and penises, it's a bit more like the fall-out from the Francis Bacon craze that you used to see a lot in the dreadful lost sad semi-figurative art of, say,

Jake and Dinos Chapman *'Chapmanworld'* (detail) 1997

Paris in the 60s and 70s, when they really didn't know what the hell they were doing or what the main international stream of art was. But of course never quite that bad.

It's never quite that bad partly because the same ironic goo that lands on the Chapmans lands inevitably on all the other Britpop artists too, in small or large plops. But also partly because the times are different now and for some reason the Existentialist beatnik Bohemian subjects suddenly seem genuinely quite good. So in the end what will really turn out to have been good about Britpop was that it rehabilitated Bohemianism and my parents.

All smiles

Sarah Lucas

Sarah Lucas and Tracey Emin

One day in the early 90s, when I was on the way to the block of sub-sidized artists' studios where I had a space for about twelve years, I decided to stop off at Sarah Lucas's and Tracey Emin's shop in Bethnal Green Road. I didn't know either of them personally and until this moment had never heard of Tracey Emin.

Sarah Lucas is famous now for artworks that at first seem like nothing more than crudely made sex symbols. Tin cans bent into a cock and balls shape. A packet of kippers or a plastic bucket standing for a vagina. A stream of variations on that. They seem so crudely and starkly done, so deliberately un-artlike, you can't believe that's all they are. You feel the crudeness must be some kind of metaphor in itself. It must be about something subtler and harder to get than the mere black humorous sex symbol on offer. Something about modern life, known to us all, but not expressed before, that could only be expressed in this way. I think that's it.

She had recently had a show at the artists-run City Racing Gallery – so-called because the space was previously a betting shop, near the Oval in South London – called 'Penis Nailed To A Board'. The title work was a rough looking board game made of clippings from a newspaper article.

The article was about a mutual mutilation sex scandal, where a group of homosexual mutilators had received prison sentences even though they'd agreed to be mutilated because they liked it. Another work was a large photo-collage of what looked like a close-up of a bowl of soup, with a lot of cut-out shapes of photos of tips of real penises floating in it. Also there was a wooden construction thing crudely attached to the top of an upturned real bicycle, as if the bicycle just happened to be there and it was a convenient thing to attach a wooden construction to. And attached to the construction were snapshot photos of the naked torso of a pale man with his head cropped, holding phallic-shaped vegetables over his crotch. There was also an eight-foot-wide enlargement of a page from the *Sunday Sport* featuring sex dwarves.

Sarah Lucas *Two Fried Eggs and a Kebab* 1992

Sarah Lucas *Sod You Gits* 1990

Soon after, she was in a group show which was scattered around various non-art venues in Soho, which I never saw but I'd heard it also featured a work of hers, a table with some fried eggs and a kebab on it. When I saw this very same work later in the Saatchi Gallery, it was clear the eggs and kebab and table made up a kind of obscene schematized female body. But before that I thought the work sounded good anyway, just because of its ingredients and the fact that it was in Soho, where you might expect to get a kebab.

Anyway, I walked into the shop and there they were, all smiles, Tracey Emin's a bit strangely toothy. They said they liked my bicycle, which was blue. I asked them what they were selling and they showed me some Damien Hirst ashtrays and some T-shirts with the words Complete Arsehole roughly hand-painted on them, and some Sarah Lucas mobiles,

Tracey Emin and **Sarah Lucas**'s shop in Bethnal Green Road

Sarah Lucas

Tracey Emin

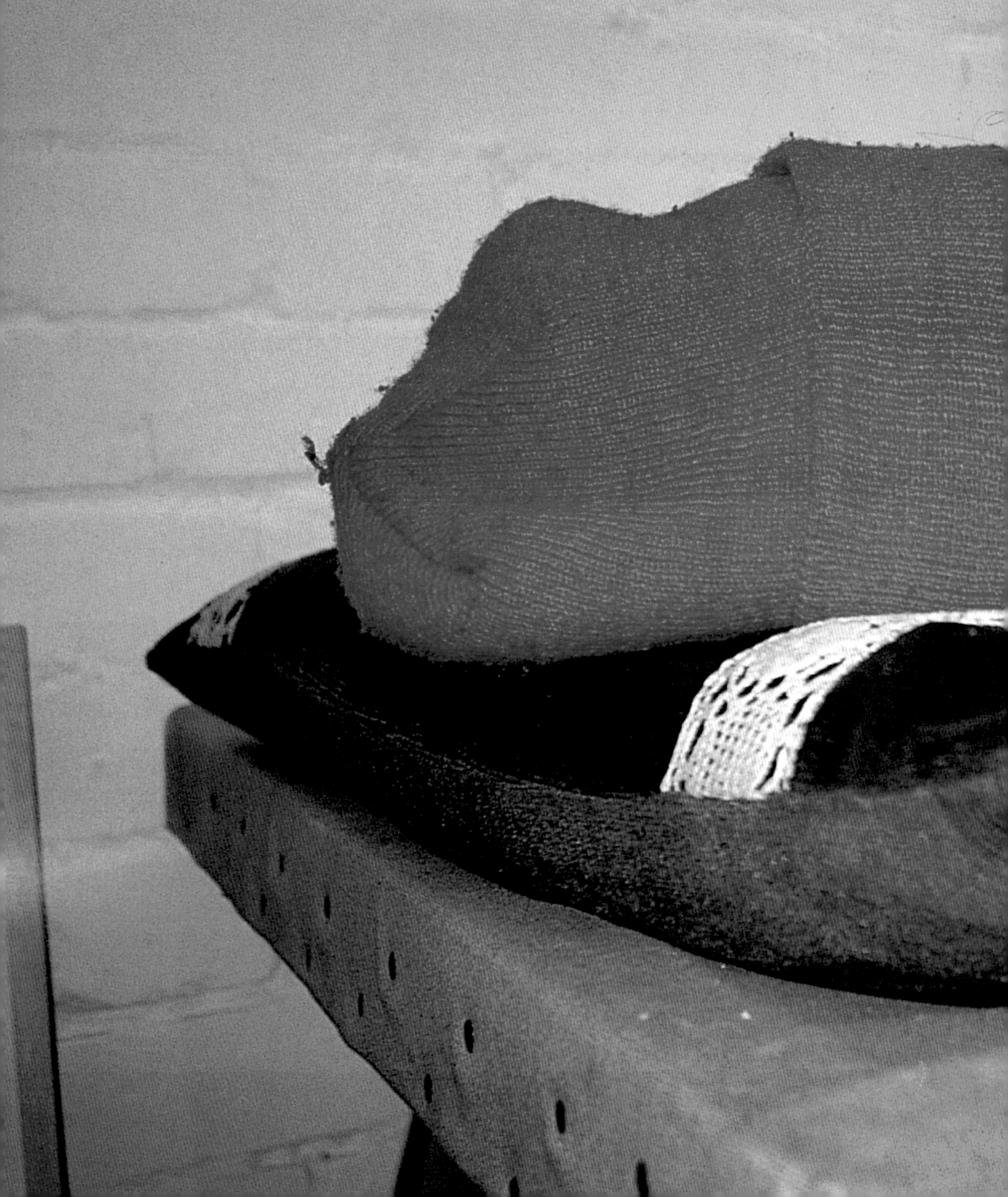

made of photos of herself sitting on a chair in jeans and T-shirt and Doc Martens, with the photos hanging by threads of cotton from a flimsy wire mobile structure. The mobiles were £50 each. I couldn't tell if that was expensive or cheap, so I bought one anyway. It lasted about two years before the thread came undone and then it got tangled up.

They said there was a Happening occurring at the shop on Wednesday, when some people would be coming round to wear false beards and do life drawings. Would I come? I said I would. But when the day came I was afraid, and the next time I went round there was a sign on the door saying 'Shop closed, gone to Mexico'.

After that I would see Tracey Emin at various gallery openings. She would just launch right into talking about herself in a way that would have been strange if it was anyone else, and actually was quite strange when she did it, but she did it so often it began to seem normal. Which in a way is the story of her art. At an opening at Maureen Paley's gallery, Interim Art, in Beck Road, she said she'd studied art first but then given it up and studied philosophy. She seemed really set on making it in the

Tracey Emin *My Major Retrospective 1982–1992*

Tracey Emin with her bag

artworld. Then she took a tooth out, I'm not sure where from, maybe her mouth, and showed it to me. I can't remember what her tooth story was, but later she seemed to have a full set, so perhaps it was about how she was going to get a new one fixed when she was successful.

And then suddenly she had a big one-person show at White Cube, the gallery in Duke Street St James run by Jay Jopling, who was Damien Hirst's agent, now his gallerist. This was the new hot gallery, and there she was. Made it. The exhibition had all the Expressionist paintings she'd been doing at Maidstone College of Art, when she was a student there, reduced to postage-stamp-size photographs, with each picture displayed on its own little shelf, all on one wall. That's a brilliant way of accepting your unacceptable past, I thought, in that therapy psychobabble way of thinking that we do now.

On the other walls, completely filling them up, was an extensive collection of incredibly student-like memorabilia. Diaries, old cigarette packets. Loads of things. A blanket or a tapestry, with the names of her relatives on it, hand-sewn, with messages to them, like, I Love You Plum, to her grandmother.

The exhibition told her life story in notes and diary and memorabilia form. It was a story which seemed tragic and hard and mostly set in Margate, with a disturbing streak of sexual abjection running through it. But it was full of passion and striving and liveliness. It was a good idea to do art that had a lot of feelings and warmth but some irony too.

He is a very good critic

Today I went into the Anthony d'Offay Gallery on Dering Street and saw an installation there by the deaf American artist Joseph Grigely. It was all the bits of paper that he and other people had written on, during the course of a meal, instead of talking. One piece of paper read:

Juan Munoz is a friend of Adrian Searle
a critic in London
he is a very good critic
funny in the 70s he did a lot drugs and a bit of S&M

Adrian Searle

Tuesdays are good

Of course that was really about Juan Munoz the Spanish artist and not Adrian Searle, *The Guardian*'s very good regular art writer. Life seems really worth living on Tuesday mornings now, when you get *The Guardian* and turn to the arts pages and there's a double page spread of visual arts reviews with colour pictures and one of his articles, or even two sometimes, and those little inserts where an artist of the moment, like the Chapman brothers, say, is saying why they like a museum masterpiece like Seurat's *Bathers* in the National Gallery, or a painting by Bellini. In the old days you would never think of reading those pages in a serious way, but now you do.

The Situationists in London

Then I went out into the street and saw the art writer, Andrew Wilson. What shall I put in this book about the London artworld, I asked him. He said, Er, Situationists in London, who was the main one? Ralph Rumney, I answered. Wrong, he said, Alexander Trocchi. *Cain's Book*, I said. Yeah, he said. And as I got into my car, he called out, Who burned *Cain's Book*? I said I didn't know. He cried: John Latham! But I thought he ate Clement Greenberg's book.

More Chapmans

But before all that happened we had been talking about shocks in art, and whether that was the route to deep content or not. He said it was extraordinary how unshocking the Chapman brothers' art used to be, only a few years ago. They used to do Minimalism parodies, like everyone else. So I made my confession to him about the legend of Jake. And he said it was Dinos too, they'd both been beaten up. Then after that they started being shocking.

Situationism

Under the paving stones, the beach! That's what the Situationists used to cry. But I don't know anything at all about the Situationists in London. I read *Cain's Book*, like you probably, when I was thirteen, which in my case was in 1968, Situationism's top year. The movement began in

Paris in the 50s. It was about revolutionizing daily life. *Cain's Book* was a depressing read, about masturbation in Soho, and heroin and encounters with ragged prostitutes for a charge of ten shillings, or 1/6d, or whatever it was at the time he was writing about. The post-war period. I didn't know that was Situationism, or that Alexander Trocchi was one.

Film itself

If he was, he would have been excommunicated, as all the Situationists gradually were, one by one, by the leader in Paris, Guy Debord, who wrote *The Society of the Spectacle*, the main Situationist book, and who had made Situationist films, which were about film itself, before he gave up making things. Or maybe Alexander Trocchi was the only one who wasn't.

Blimey

When it was the twentieth anniversary of 1968, there was a memorial exhibition of Situationism at the ICA that had come over from the Pompidou Centre in Paris, where Situationism began, and there were a lot of seminars and articles and even TV films on the subject. For a while the Situationists were really exciting. They *dérived* and *détourned*.

Détourning is Situationists writing their own words – the thoughts of Chairman Mao, say – in the speech balloons of teenage girls' romance comics. *Dériving* is walking around the city not obeying the usual walking habits, or even the traffic lights, and crying to the other Situationists *dériving* along with you, Blimey mate we're in a parallel universe!

Then the Situationists would go home and make maps with directional arrows pointing nowhere, and the maps were called Urban Psycho-geographies.

The Situationists had something to do with Malcolm McLaren, or at least they didn't really, but gradually we all had to agree that they did, even though inside you nursed your private doubt because, let's face it, he always seems a bit tiresome.

It is striking how silly and ephemeral everything the original Situationists did and said was, but how abiding their impact has been, how their legend goes on rippling and echoing. Somehow you can really believe that Young British art now is more or less in the parallel universe too. Do we want to join it there? We don't know.

Then the other day Guy Debord, the leader, finally committed suicide, after being authentically underground, hiding from the CIA, for two decades. They wanted to get the secret of film itself. But nobody really noticed and Alexander Trocchi is probably dead too now.

Bar du Marché

Then after I left Andrew Wilson I went to Bar du Marché in Berwick Street and had a marinated chicken salad and read *The Face*. Blow me if there wasn't an article about the Chapman brothers in there! There were pictures of their new sculptures of children mannequins horribly fused into grotesque children clusters, with sore looking erections poking through. Which they were going to show at their forthcoming ICA exhibition. Also the brothers were pictured painting their new paintings, which seemed to be on paper, with casual looking drawings and writings crowding the white space, like Jean-Michel Basquiat, the New York grafitti artist of the 80s who died.

R.B. Kitaj *Clinton* 1996

Artist draws Prez

In the paper today it says Kitaj has just been over to Washington to do a portrait of Bill Clinton for Oxford University. What a guy! I'm really on his side in the debate, whatever the debate is.

Sarah Lucas and Tracey Emin II

So anyway, after the show at Jay Jopling, there was Tracey Emin in all the big shows, like Gary Hume and Jake and Dinos Chapman, her position assured. Lower than Damien Hirst, as everyone is. But higher than the twins, Jane and Louise Wilson, say. Or, if you were

Tracey Emin
Everyone I Have Ever Slept With
1963–1995 1995

thinking more in terms of a pulsating circle, with Damien Hirst at the centre, then she would be further out than Sarah Lucas, but further in than the twins and Georgina Starr and Gavin Turk, say. Maybe pulsating with the same level of glow as Gary Hume and Mark Wallinger. Maybe slightly more radiant that Gillian Wearing. Or maybe both their pulsations are equal but alternating.

But really the Damien Hirst centre is a complicated idea now, since he doesn't seem to be trying so hard any more and only over-produces, without any development in quality.

In a show called 'Minky Manky' in the South London Art Gallery, organized by her boyfriend at that time, the art writer Carl Freedman, Tracey Emin showed a real tent with the names of everyone she had ever slept with embroidered on it, called *Everyone I Have Ever Slept With 1963 – 1995*. She also published a book called *Explorations of the Soul*, which was a book of stories about her growing-up pains and the adventures of her brother Paul. The stories have a great style with good opening thoughts, like 'I didn't mind it when Paul head-butted me and knocked my front teeth out, as I never smiled much anyway… '. She's always going round the world, doing readings from the book and showing her embroideries. In the desert, in hotels, in the private homes of rich collectors.

Then suddenly there was a Tracey Emin museum, run by herself, in Waterloo. It seemed right that there should be one, even though with anyone else it would seem embarassing. For example, a few years ago I stumbled across a kind of self-museum in New York run by Ernst Niesvestny, the Russian artist John Berger once wrote a briefly celebrated book about, in the 60s. I think it was called *An Artist of Our Time*. This museum in the middle of SoHo, New York's art gallery playground, seemed a hopeless, sad affair, inadvertently symbolizing the defeat of idealism by consumerism, and everything becoming the society of the spectacle. Rather than the happy, positive affairs that Tracey Emin's museum, and her other activities, have been.

Tracey Emin's museum

Tracey Emin's museum

Tracey Emin's museum

Tracey Emin opening her museum

Jane and Louise Wilson
Normapaths 1995

What other museums like this have there been? Not many. It's just not something that can be pulled off in the normal run of things.

So with all this happening she was soon seen as a separate entity from Sarah Lucas. They appeared together in a film on TV once, laughing and being drunk in their shop. And the odd postcard would come through the door with them pictured both together, each holding a pair of melons, and a caption saying, Cor, what a pair, or Big Ones. Or something in the *Carry On* style that Sarah Lucas ironically appropriates. But now they mostly soar separately.

Train of meaning

I saw Tracey Emin and Sarah Lucas once at a seminar on art held at the Royal Academy. It was sponsored by Belgo, the restaurant, and free Belgian beers were given out. They each presented slide-shows of their work and then answered questions from the audience, which was made up of collectors, dealers, museum-curators and writers. The questions were

idiotic and the replies were inane, but everyone present laughed and sighed delightedly anyway, like it was an audience with the Bhagwan.

But all seminars about Young British art are like that. It's like being stuck behind children or old or blind people in a crowd at an underground station, when you're trying to hurry for the train.

The twins

The twins' christian names were Jane and Louise. They exhibited under the name Jane Wilson and Louise Wilson. They did spooky photographs and videos of themselves in out of the ordinary situations, like being hypnotized in a seedy motel off a highway in America, or taking their first acid trip in a darkened room, in Vienna I think it was, with a strobe light flickering.

There was a consistency of atmosphere to everything they did. It was always spooky and groovy. They looked groovy at all times, in real life

Jane and Louise Wilson
Normapaths 1995

and in their art. In conversation they were normal, with down-to-earth up-north accents, although rather speedy and exhaustingly eager to please and to be lively and flip whatever the situation. One was slightly more speedy and wired-up seeming than the other. But if you were talking to the less wired one on her own, you would just think, she's really wired, she should calm down. It was only when they were together that you could grade their wiredness.

Once they had two exhibitions at the same time. One was at the new Milch Gallery off Charing Cross Road which replaced the old Milch Gallery in Great Russell Street, which closed down after the director Lawren Mabel died after running off with all the money. This exhibition was called 'Crawl Space' and it was a film of a spooky dark house, with unclear horror film things happening, like somebody being dragged up some stairs, and one special effect, where a bubble of light floated around the room. Maybe there was a twin in it trying to escape. I don't remember.

The other film was at the Chisenhale Gallery in the East End and was part of an installation that had the set of the film, a whole room with bits of broken things lying around, in one part of the gallery, and the film itself in another part. The film was projected from two projectors onto a corner of the gallery, so that the action was divided between the two corners. The twins were in the film, which is quite short, and also there were two other twin-size women, all of them in Avengers-like cat-suits. They ran around a warehouse type of space and fought each other, in a highly stylized Avengers-like way, as if they were in a Kung Fu film. There was a fire. Then the twins were reaching out their hands to each other, but when the shot went to a close-up the hands were actually their feet, which was creepy.

At the end of the 'Crawl Space' film, the camera was in a locked-off position, showing one of the twins lying down with her belly exposed, and the flesh of the belly gradually blistering up into the words CRAWL SPACE, as if they had been burned there by invisible laser beams.

Although there always seemed to be a lot of coverage of the twins' activities, it was never very clear what the meaning of what they did was. Or if they were really respected as artists. They were in a lot of group shows in London and abroad, but somehow not quite in so many that you felt their status was absolutely assured. There was an undercurrent of suspicion about them, as if they had only got their success by being twins. It seemed a bit too easy that they were women and a duo, two automatically good things to be in the artworld.

Jane and Louise Wilson
Hypnotic Suggestion '505' 1993

But then they went to Germany on a D.A.A.D. scholarship. This is a top art prize involving a generous grant and a spacious studio and a good flat to live in, given by the German government, which Damien Hirst once had. They were a bit nervous about it before they went. No doubt they were torn between feeling they ought to rush on with consolidating their position here, having yet more shows, and feeling that a year abroad would lead to big international recognition, so their position here would just take care of itself.

But maybe they weren't thinking those things at all, but were just worried about missing their mum, who they introduced to me at the Chisenhale Gallery, and who was just like Damien Hirst's mum, who did a brilliant turn in a BBC film about him once.

Art & Language II

Art & Language, the Conceptual art group, started up in the art school in Coventry in the 60s, where the members of the group who were teaching there would hold a lot of seminars about meaning, and the students would all get really frightened or bored or else inspired and want to join Art & Language themselves. The group's exhibitions were of filing cabinets with index cards recording the group's inquiries into meaning. They published a magazine that no one could understand. Gradually the group got a bit larger and spread to New York, and then after a few years some of the New York members fell out with the members in England.

Art & Language *Index 04* 1973–74

And after that the New York members considered that the group was finished but the ones in England thought it was still going on, and maybe just to aggravate the ones in New York they started doing Art & Language paintings on canvas with oil paints, with a lot of busy energetic brush-marks, which was like worshipping Satan because of course painting had always been completely out. They set problems for themselves. For example, they did one set of paintings entirely by mouth, to test theories of expression.

Michael Baldwin of **Art & Language**

These paintings went on and on into the 90s, and with them the Art & Language reputation for utter terrifying intellectuality gradually waned. But when they were doing Conceptual art in the 60s and 70s, there was no one more rigorous and frightening and impenetrable than them.

But they weren't only impenetrable, they were often grimly funny. They once published a critique of John Berger, which took apart, almost literally sentence by sentence, his book *Ways of Seeing*, based on his TV

Art & Language
*Portrait of V.I. Lenin in the Style
of Jackson Pollock, V* 1980

series of the same name. The book pointed out, incredibly pedantically, how patronizing and middle-class and pompous and pretentious and generally gittish John Berger is. Things which most people, including me, hadn't particularly worried about before. But now it's impossible not to notice them. On the cover of their book was the famous Magritte painting where ordinary objects are surrealistically incorrectly labelled. But instead of the horse being labelled *The Clock*, say, it was labelled *The Walter Benjamin*. When they wanted to simplify a logical proposition by making children ask questions of each other, as John Berger might do, rather than calling the children Janet and John, they called them middle-class names like Electra and Jason, or Tristram.

Return of documenting everything

In the 60s and 70s Conceptual artists always documented everything. Then documenting things was out. But then it came back again in the 90s. Although Gilbert & George had documented themselves being drunk, in such loopy early 70s works as *Floating* and *Slipping Glasses* and *Gordon's Makes Us Drunk*, on the whole by the late 70s the general documenting craze came to be associated with an uninspired, plodding or phoney approach. So when it came back, as everything comes back, it was the loopy side of documenting that was favoured, not the dry side.

Those documentarists

The main one is Gillian Wearing, a top documentarist artist of the 90s. For her work *Confessions*, which was shown at Interim Art a few years ago, she placed an ad in *Loot* asking for anyone who wanted to confess something to phone her up. Some ordinary people answered the ad and were invited to come round to a room and be filmed doing their confessions. Many of the confessions were smutty. Only the last confessor in the film seemed really disturbed and should possibly have been in hospital. Part of the appeal of *Confessions* was the grotesque joke shop masks the confessors had been given to wear, to conceal their

Andrea and **Philippe** with Fîla

Adam Chodzko

Bob and Roberta Smith

Jessica Voorsanger and Etta

Gillian Wearing *Dancing in Peckham* 1994

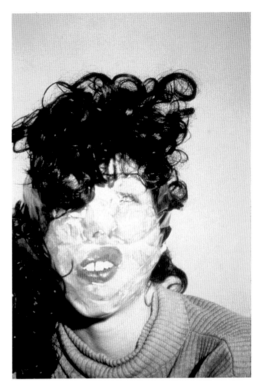

Gillian Wearing *Confess All on Video* 1994

identities. Or maybe it wasn't just part of the appeal but the main thing that made it work at all as art.

Lucy Gunning has documented some women imitating the sound of horses neighing, and some other women playing football in a small flat in their shorts. Andrea and Philippe document themselves going around the country glazing the windows of World War II pillboxes. Adam Chodzko has documented ordinary people who think they might look like God. Jeremy Deller has documented his search for Bez, the dancer in the Manchester band The Happy Mondays, who couldn't play any instruments. Angela Bulloch has documented some Japanese people. And Gary Hume has documented himself having a bath with all his clothes on and smoking cigarettes, in a film with the anagramatic title *King Cnut*. Jessica Voorsanger is a psycho celebrity artist who documents herself tracking down slightly sad media celebrities like David Cassidy or Tony Slattery and trying to get them to write to her. Patrick Brill, who exhibits under the pseudonym Bob and Roberta Smith, has done a wide range of documenting works, including video documentation of himself learning Italian from a cassette, and another one called *Humiliate,* where he tells true stories to the camera about his failure to make it in the artworld.

Turnips

Patrick Brill does a lot of other art as well as video tapes, all frankly idiotic, but always funny, including concrete casts of real turnips coated with gloss paint, and toy sailing boats made of concrete. He also makes up rambling stories that mix together in nonsense situations important figures from different cultural areas. Voltaire, Kurt Cobain and Clement Greenberg all meeting in a record shop, for example. The stories, which are painted in wonky capital letters in gloss paint on old boards, have a ranting angry edge which suggests a level of protest somewhere. He also runs a Rock band called, painfully, The Ken Ardley Playboys.

Gary Hume *Me as King Cnut* 1995

Insulting

Do you know how to relate to curators, art writers, art professionals etc. if you are an artist? Always make them feel good about themselves by flattering them and saying how good you thought the last thing they published or organized or whatever, was. Then subtly put down the work of all other artists, so they gradually think yours is really good and they imagine they thought of it themselves.

If you are a writer or curator, you will find this behaviour insulting on all sorts of levels, but somehow also soothing. That's probably the same for a lot of social interactions in the artworld.

He never said
he wouldn't

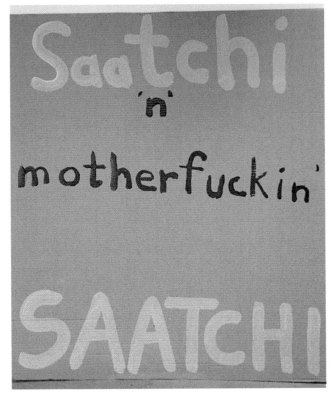

Colin Lowe and **Roddy Thomson** *Saatchi n' motherfuckin Saatchi* 1996

The word Saatchi

Last night I called into a fund-raising event at the artists-run Cubitt Street Studios behind Kings Cross. It was a tombola. Everyone who had paid £30 for a ticket won a work of art. The works were donated by all the artists who had ever shown in the gallery at Cubitt Street. Many of these artists are good. One of the works to be won was a small chunky canvas with the word Saatchi roughly painted once along the top edge of the canvas and once again along the bottom edge. In the space between the two Saatchis it said: 'n'motherfuckin'. Everyone liked it. It was by two artists, Colin Lowe and Roddy Thomson.

The jokey rage of this painting, its sputtering incoherence, its ejaculation, was an effective expression of a strange artworld phenomenon. The way the word is so loaded, so guaranteed to provoke groaning and eyeball rolling, but at the same time nobody can ever quite sum up what the problem is. Or even, often, who it is they're dealing with.

It's not Saatchi & Saatchi who buys art, but Charles Saatchi. It used to be Doris and Charles Saatchi. But now it's just him. On the other hand his company buys art too. And maybe his brother does too. And maybe Doris still does too. And maybe his current wife, who used to work in an art gallery, does too. And maybe it's Charles Saatchi who buys the art for his company. And is it still his company? And do they still buy art? He buys more art than anyone else in the country, maybe in the world. And everything is different because of that. But how much different? And for the worse or the better? Is it bad or clever that he tries to get knock-down prices? Is he a bully or nice? Why is it bad if he sells a lot of his art? He never said he wouldn't. Or maybe he did.

And his regular round-up exhibitions of his new purchases – good or bad? Sophisticated or crass? What about those catalogues he gets written for his shows, by Sarah Kent, the *Time Out* regular art critic? Blimey they're boring. Except they're not if you're in them.

Also, all those things about rage etc., that I described about the painting, are quite interesting or worth saying some more about, in terms of artists doing works nowadays that are both sincere and alienated. The young artists have inherited alienated art forms, that were originally designed

Saatchi Gallery

to negate or suppress feeling, but they use them to express feeling. This can be bad when they do crying on video, which is always a bit desperate and corny, but bound to be noticed. But it can be good when they use the ambiguity to express feelings that actually are ambiguous.

What did I mean by that?

What would be an example of an ambiguous feeling successfully expressed in an alienated form? I can't think of one now. Unless it's all the alienated forms, except the ones that have crying.

Slut over

Adrian Searle was rolling the bits of paper round the tombola and announcing the names of the winners, which was everybody, and which artist they'd won a work by. When he called out the name of Andrew Renton, the art writer, he said Andrew Rentboy. And when it was the turn of Matthew Slotover, one of the editors of *frieze*, the art magazine, he said Matthew Slutover.

The authors of the Saatchi n'motherfuckin Saatchi painting do other works in the same vein. In the correspondence pages of the current *Art Monthly* they have an almost believable letter, full of sputtering rage about an innaccuracy that might have been in the last issue. Only the letter is so raging it's impossible to tell what the innacuracy was.

Adam Chodzko

Adam Chodzko does a kind of art that seems to be on a constant alert for bits of everyday life experience that haven't yet been used for art. Recently he started recording video film of himself setting off distress flares in a forest onto the blank bit of tape at the end of rented video movies. The credits would have rolled by, you'd be not particularly concentrating, or maybe half asleep, and then suddenly there he would be on your TV screen, firing off distress flares in a forest.

Adam Chodzko *From Beyond* (detail) 1996

The Devils

Another private view. In the car afterwards there is a discussion about the category of art that Adam Chodzko fits. Is it Conceptual? Cries of derision. Why not? Just more cries. Perhaps Conceptual is too high. But artists are always a bit bitter about other artists' success.

What was in the exhibiton we were just at anyway? Everybody in the car remembers Adam Chodzko's film in the basement that was clips from Ken Russell's film *The Devils*, with the surviving extras who'd played bit parts in the nun sex devil worship scenes, all appearing again in their new old look of the 90s while behind them their young nude selves of the 70s romped, worshipping the arch fiend. Documentary art! the triumphant cry goes up.

But wait, one person paid careful attention to his works on the ground floor too. We all noticed a road map on a table that had a blob of molten glass with veins of red liquid running through it, the veins relating, perhaps, who knows, to the streets on the map. But our observant undrunken driver had been looking carefully at the photos on the walls too, and noticed the scenes, which were of roof-tops and also of private hand-written letters from people answering personal column ads lying thrown away in wet grass, and she had noticed that the roof-top scenes were viewed through spider webs that had blood on them. Uh? Incoherent gurgling sounds as we speed through the winding East End streets to a warehouse show called 'Flag.'

Andrew Renton

The Adam Chodzko private view was at another new Euro gallery in the West End called Lotta Hammer. But it was also partly in the adjacent building which was a new gallery run by the art writer Andrew Renton. He said it wasn't really a gallery, but a Projects Space. I forgot to ask him for some topics for this book. Both spaces were completely packed with people, they spilled out onto the street, drinking their beers and posing and making their witty comments.

Flag

At this new warehouse show it's also crowded and beer-ridden. There are many people exhibiting. In a cellar there's a film flickering and a light box with slides on it. The slides are all photos of rubbish. Outside in the street there's a blue plastic bag with sand in it and a steel chain securing the bag to the outside brick wall of the warehouse space, and a label on the wall that says *Plastic, Sand, Steal*. Back inside I see Keith Arnatt, the Conceptual artist of the 70s who photographed himself some time in that decade or even earlier, disappearing into a hole in the ground in stages, and another time photographed himself with the caption, I am an artist. Or maybe it was the same time. His son Matthew Arnatt is now grown up and after a career in advertising has become an artist. It's him who tells me that steal isn't a misprint. I know I am naïve, I hope he didn't notice, and thought I was just being obscurely droll when I said it was misspelled. At another private view at the ICA the other night the artist Henry Bond, who has done a lot of different things including pretending to be a press photographer with Liam Gillick and going to official press events, like Kylie Minogue opening a shop, or Gordon Brown giving a speech, and then exhibiting the photos as art, was laughing at what he saw as the naïvety of some artist or other and it wasn't even her show. Then he said he himself had never done any art that was of any interest whatsoever, and I couldn't tell if he was having a crisis and if I should say something reassuring, or if he was boasting.

Giorgio Sadotti

I go up to Giorgio Sadotti and say Hi! brightly and ask him where his flag is, as all the works in 'Flag' are flags, even the plastic bag work and the slides of rubbish. They're all flags but you can't see how. When I find Giorgio's work it's a polaroid photo of a room seen through the arch of Giorgio's – I assume it's his – naked crotch, showing a red-painted, or maybe just naturally red, scrotum. Maybe it's a red flag. At the Cubitt Street Gallery just now he has the remains of a meal given for artists and art professionals, like writers and museum people, displayed as an artwork. The artists all contributed things to the meal, like recipes or artworks, and the art professionals all ate it.

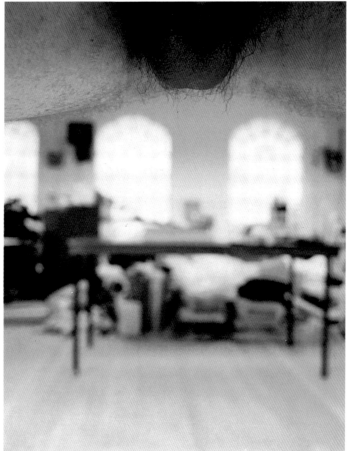

Giorgio Sadotti *Giorgio's Balls* 1997

Tragedy of now

Today I read in *The Art Newspaper*, an international artworld news magazine designed like an actual newspaper, like *The Times* from 1964, say, to symbolize that only hard-headed information about concrete realities and not airy intellectualizing will be on the menu, that Rachel Whiteread has been commissioned to do a holocaust memorial in Austria. Wow, that'll certainly give some relief to holocaust survivors.

In *The Guardian's* TV review column recently, the reviewer was complaining about a TV programme where the journalist Cosmo Landesman took it

PETER REP⌐   AH DOIG
ALTHOFF VAN   ⌐A'GER
UNDER THA⌐   ⌐HA⌐ EE⌐
'IRON MAID⌐   J SMITH⌐
'CLEANING K⌐   ⌐CHENS' H⌐
TURRELL, D⌐   G + MEK
'MAKEOVE⌐   ⌐CRAN

MIROS⌐
'MAC⌐
BASQ⌐
JASP⌐
'TOP GE⌐
'HILL⌐
WOBE⌐
DUCH⌐
OMEA⌐
NAU⌐
TORR⌐
'RESE⌐
O.R.'⌐
HALL⌐
'ON'⌐
THOM⌐
H♥Y⌐
WEIS⌐
RICHA⌐
PEOP⌐
B. 9Q⌐
LL MI⌐

Pete Davies

for granted that Damien Hirst and Rachel Whiteread were charlatans. But surely, the reviewer asked, all earnest, these artists have something important to say about how we live and die?

Do they really have something important to say about those things? They both keep the issues rolling as art issues, which is an achievement. But we can't tell yet how important are the things that they seem to be saying. A cast is just a cast, is another thing they might be saying. A butterfly is just a butterfly. A cow a cow. A house a house.

This is art that comes from a particular climate, with a particular build-up of attitudes and ideas behind it, and although poetry and metaphor play their part, and other high-minded things, you can't just remove facetiousness and irony and emptiness from the equation when it suits you. When you're feeling a bit solemn. That's the tragedy of now.

Also there's an article about the Chapman brothers' mannequins. Could they be sued for copyright infringement by the original designers of the shop-bought mannequins they stick erect penises on?

Die Yuppie Scum

Today I saw an exhibition curated by Martin Maloney called 'Die Yuppie Scum'. It was a pretentious title since no artists really want to exterminate yuppies, they want them to buy their art too much, unless it was a clever Anglo-German collective noun for the artists in the show.

Martin Maloney's own paintings were in the exhibition and they were straightforward colourful oil paintings of flowers, with an art student look. Loose and bold. They seemed ordinarily nice and it was confusing because you wondered if there was a strategy, and if there wasn't, what were they doing in this show, which had a lot of ironic art in it?

top: **Martin Maloney** *Hyacinths in a Bowl* 1996
bottom: **Martin Maloney** *Grape Hyacinths* 1996

Pete Davies *Text Painting* (detail) 1996

Making things disappear

For example, also in 'Die Yuppie Scum' was a work by Pete Davies, a painting of written sentences in cartoon letters, with the letters in different colours and the sentences describing all the art that Pete Davies is thinking of. Contemporary trendies, like Sigmar Polke and Damien Hirst. But also heroic early Modernists and some pre-Moderns. The thoughts were funny hip one-liner descriptions.

The first artist on the list was Sean Landers. The painting as a whole was an appropriation of Sean Landers' writing/painting style, with some of the laughs of Sean Landers but not the neurotic self-examination and sudden double-takes that make Sean Landers uniquely noticeable in a world of young white male abject comedy art.

But Sean Landers has only been on the scene for about ten minutes and it seems a bit quick off the mark to be re-doing him, or robbing his soul, or challenging him, or laughing along with him, or whatever it is that this painting is doing with him.

Martin Maloney

Historically

Historically, or recent-historically, historically from about 1960, say, this direct robbery mode, where the robber tries to keep his spirits up by taking over the voice that intimidates him, tends to have the effect of summing up everything about the stolen subject, in a way that makes the subject disappear.

Like the way Jasper Johns' 1960 painting of two wooden balls jammed between some hinged-together canvases with abstract expressionist-type brushstrokes on them seemed to sum up the problematic macho-ness of Abstract Expressionism and make Abstract Expressionism disappear. Everybody knew about that macho-ness in those days of course, but before Jasper Johns nobody thought of expressing it in the form of an artwork, only in the form of off-the-record bitter private view sneers.

To make an artwork out of an aside was a good idea. It opened the door for things like Roy Lichtenstein's paintings of huge dripping brushstrokes done in Ben Day dots, and Andy Warhol. That was when Jasper Johns was good. Now nobody copies him any more. Although he's famous for being the most expensive living artist at auctions, even more than de Kooning.

So now it must be that everyone knows about Sean Landers and feels the weight of his presence, as strongly as the New York neo-Dadaists and Popists of the late 50s felt the weight of Abstract Expressionism. And now Pete Davies has summed up Sean Landers and made him disappear, which is a shame as he was so good. And now someone will have to make Pete Davies disappear, but they'll have to do it in. 05 of a second to keep up with the new pace.

We should paint her

The time John Latham ate Clement Greenberg's book was the 1960s, when John Latham was teaching at St Martin's. He ate the book partly himself but also got his students to help eat it. They didn't completely eat it but ate as much as they could and then returned some of the masticated pages, which John Latham then made into an organic culture, because the book was called *Art and Culture*. It was from the school

John Latham

library. When the library wrote to him later asking for the book back, he returned the culture in a jar and then he was sacked from the school.

He was a nutty professor type. Once, in the 80s, I watched him perform in front of a large audience at Riverside Studios. He batted some tennis balls that had been dipped in black paint at a white canvas, and when he'd finished, it was a painting. Then a team of real professors from Oxford and Cambridge, who he'd had bussed in for the event, discussed the painting with him in terms of theories of Time and Space.

With his wife, Barbara Steveni, he used to run the Artists' Placement Group, which had an office at Riverside Studios. This was a project to place artists in industry. Stuart Brisley, the performance artist of the 70s, was placed in industry once. I don't know what he did there. Barbara Steveni said John Latham had been in a terrible car or motorbike accident once and all his bones were broken and he was in hospital being repaired for a long time.

Stuart Brisley made a cage once, not in industry but in the Serpentine Gallery, with some gloves in it that he got from London Transport. There were 66 gloves, each filled with plaster. They stood for the 666,000 people who were out of work in 1984, or some time in the 80s. Maybe it wasn't the Serpentine Gallery. I know Mona Hatoum had a cage there in the 90s, and it was about political prisoners or Beckettian loneliness or something, and then it turned up again in the exhibition of Turner Prize nominees for 1995.

Mona Hatoum was at the Byam Shaw art school when I was there in the 70s. She had just come to London from Beirut. There was another artist from Beirut in my year who went mad and took all her clothes off in a life class and said we should paint her.

Glistening highlights

Nicholas May

Who are the artists of now?

Nicholas May. Pete Davies. That's two of them. One came up to me in the canteen at Chelsea art school the other day. It was Nicholas May. I was there with my mother. He was sorry I'd missed his private view at Victoria Miro but was happy that Charles Saatchi had just bought most of the paintings from his show. And I suppose it was the devil in me, but I laughed and asked if he had sold them yet.

But then I was sorry when I saw the look of genuine dismay come over him, and he really did start visibly racking his brains and trying to work out if the paintings had all been crated off to Saatchi's or if they'd been labelled for some international dealer in Switzerland or somewhere. And I tried to make up for this cruelty but the damage was done.

Nicholas May

I first met Nicholas May when I was working for the BBC and there was some filming being done about Goldsmiths College, looking at the explosion of interest in artists who had attended the BA and MA courses at the College that ocurred in the late 80s. Not that those exploding would have noticed there were two separate courses.

We filmed a Goldsmiths MA seminar which was being held in Nicholas May's studio. He was extremely tongue-tied and shy and there was a lot of incoherent self-conscious discussion going on amongst the rest of the artists in the MA group about his paintings, which were large abstract canvases in an exuberant but incoherent splashy style that seemed hopelessly un-80s in its looseness. Splashes and blobs in painting were just impossible then.

After that his style got much more coherent and his new paintings in the 'Young Contemporaries' exhibition at the ICA in 1989 or 90 were bought by Doris Saatchi. Although sadly they were passed on for resale a few years later and the price was very low.

Nicholas May *Formless Fold (Red)* 1994

Nicholas May

But it was very impressive the way his new style of single isolated blobs was simply a focused version of his old style, which had been many blobs and splashes in a conventional compositional arrangement that was somehow timid and ordinary. The new focused blobs looked uncanny as if it was the return of the repressed blob in a Freudian sense.

The Goldsmiths MA Course

After that I did this same MA course myself. It's really healthy, even though it might seem to an outsider, as it did to me that first time in Nicholas May's studio, a bit depressing and low powered. I mean to an outsider who would actually get to witness the course in action. Of course most outsiders, who would never get to witness the course in action but only hear about it, think of it as a hot-bed of intellectualizing, with Julia Kristeva and Jacques Lacan being quoted feverishly all the time.

Lacan and Kristeva

Lacan said the unconscious is structured like a language, and Julia Kristeva opened the doors to let the idea of abjection into the artworld, which was to take off so strongly in the 90s. Like Marshall McLuhan opened the doors for those ideas of his in the 60s, and somebody else opened the doors for Information theory, and somebody else for Chaos theory, and so on. They're great, those theories. They last for a few years and then get used up.

Siobhan Hapaska *Far* 1995

My year

There was a lot of really good artists in my year at Goldsmiths and many of these progressed to stardom directly after the course, some even during it. In fact some of those artists are the artists of now, who I was listing earlier. The Wilson twins, who we have already discussed. And Siobhan Hapaska, Glenn Brown, Carina Wiedel, who went back to Brazil, and Brad Lochore.

Siobhan Hapaska does perfectly modelled super-finished high-class sculptures of strange beds and hearts and saints, in black and white, with mysterious meanings

that nobody can fathom. Brad Lochore does pale grey and white paintings of shadows, with the shadows copied from images that he generates on a computer screen. Carina Weidel does photos of frozen chickens. And Glenn Brown does photo-realist copies of reproductions of other artist's paintings, like Salvador Dali, de Kooning and Frank Auerbach. And he does copies, sometimes very big, of science fiction illustrations, like floating asteroid cities or flying glaciers.

Not passé

Glenn Brown is one of the few artists who can still do Appropriation, which was a movement of the 80s, without it seeming *passé*. Appropriation was literally appropriating, that is, copying, other artists' images, as opposed to merely being influenced by them. It was about the death of the author and it seemed profound at first but then it was out.

Van Gogh and Rembrandt

One thing Glenn Brown does quite successfully is give new titles to his copies of paintings by Auerbach. These titles subtly relocate the Auerbach image in a world of 1950s science fiction horror imagery, which is a world of kitsch that Auerbach's imagery really does sometimes seem to inadvertently relate to. A world of nuclear holocaust and human beings turned into mutants. Whereas in the official Auerbach discourse, the Auerbach world is a world pretty much continuous with the world of van Gogh and Rembrandt and timeless values.

Glenn Brown *We'll Drink Through It All This The Modern Age* 1993

Phew

What happens when you see the Auerbach translated into a Glenn Brown, when all the huge rough intractable impasto of the furiously rendered Auerbach image is re-rendered as a cool, hyper-smooth photo-realist copy, with all the glistening highlights of Auerbach's original surface carefully copied using tiny brushes, and the title changed from, say, *Portrait of J.Y.M.*, to, say, *The Day The World Turned Auerbach*, is that you feel a great sense of relief.

Glenn Brown

Phew, the unconscious thinks, I'm glad I don't have to go around feeling slightly resentful about the official Auerbach discourse any more. And so, in a spooky way, Glenn Brown provides a health aid, like an antihistamine drug, that decongests the system. So the next time you see a real Auerbach you can think, Hmm, that's nice, without sneezing.

Gary Hume

Gary Hume is another artist of now, who was on the Goldsmiths BA, rather than the MA. In fact most of the Goldsmiths stars were on the BA rather than the MA, except for Mark Wallinger.

Mark Wallinger does multi-media art about the English class system, often using the world of horse racing as a metaphor. He is one of the few stars of now who does art about class issues. But you can't always tell that's what they are and that's good because otherwise it would be boring.

Gary Hume has always made a big effort to live down the reputation that painters have of being dull, which is an idea that goes back to Marcel Duchamp, who said, *Bête comme un peintre!* He had noticed that after a certain point the revolutionariness of, say, Picasso or Matisse or Braque, just became institutionalized and was more about bourgeois loveliness than revolutionariness. So he cleverly invented readymades, like his real urinal called *Fountain*. And that started off the idea we now have quite strongly, of modern art being divided into two main streams. One main stream is Expressionism, which always has a threat of creeping loveliness. The other one is Conceptualism, which has a threat of dryness and boredom.

At first Gary Hume painted abstracts that looked like hospital doors. They were parodies of Minimal art, but with the faint outlines of hospital doors looming through the apparently blank off-white surfaces. Then he had a crisis and came out the other side doing paintings in bright colours of lots of things from pop culture, using pictures from magazines. Teddy bears, hands and feet, big eyes, flowers, silhouette people, pictures of popular media stars like Tony Blackburn or Patsy Kensit. He found unexpected ways of making these images. Like making the face of Tony Blackburn look a bit like a four-leaf clover. And now he's the top painter of the Young British artists.

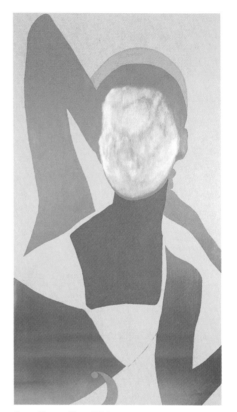

Gary Hume *More Fucking Values* 1991

Gary Hume *Kate* 1996

More artists of now

Christine Borland. I can't remember what she does. She's in an exhibition with the Chapman brothers now at the Henry Moore Foundation in Yorkshire, where they show a constant stream of exhibitions of alienated Post-Modernist type art. That's great for Henry Moore, obviously he would have really loved that.

Chris Ofili

Chris Ofili is a black painter who originally came from Manchester. He rehabilitates loose pattery decorative joyous painting, which obviously is out, even though most of us would probably quite like to paint like that, given half a chance. He rehabilitates it by placing it in a context of ethnic art and challenging our Western assumptions about ethnicity. He does dot patterns, like aborigine art, with lumps of real elephant dung stuck to the canvas, which he gets from the Zoo, and with the canvases not hanging on the wall but standing on more lumps of dung. He also gives his art an edge of hip street culture, incorporating collaged magazine images of black people with 70s Afro haircuts into his painted patterns, and making sculptures of joints.

I went to his studio the other day, in Chelsea. He came to Fulham Broadway to pick me up, driving a lime green Ford Capri and wearing wrap-around sun glasses and a pink polo-neck. Later, he was drawing some things that looked like flies arranged in a dot pattern, the pattern was gradually building up into two large oval shapes. When you looked closely you could see each dot was a little African face with an Afro hair cut. On the wall were some small canvases with more African heads done in oil paint, some with six eyes. On a table was some painting debris. There was a stack of tin foil food containers. In one of them was some breasts from a black porn magazine, cut out with scissors in irregular oval shapes, waiting to be collaged onto paintings. The sun was shining and there was a view of the Thames outside.

We were talking about the artists who run the painting departments in art schools nowadays. They tend to have the same social style, which is to act out the macho myth of the New York Abstract Expressionists of the 1940s and 50s. They get really tanked-up and then get out their

Chris Ofili in his studio

Chris Ofili

cigars and start talking in a mid-Atlantic accent about how they went to New York once and met de Kooning, or Clement Greenberg. He laughed and said that certainly sounded like his teachers at the Royal College of Art.

Gavin Turk

Gavin Turk is a young London artist who has a studio on Charing Cross Road. He does recycling art, recycling landmark works of Modernism and Post-Modernism but with a Gavin Turk twist.

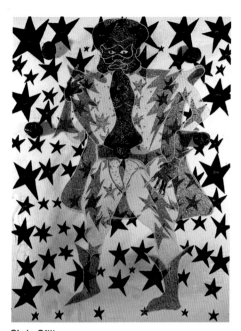

Chris Ofili
Captain Shit and the Legend of the Black Stars 1996

He recycled Piero Manzoni's signature, Marcel Duchamp's *Urinal* and Robert Morris's Minimal cubes. Piero Manzoni was a hilarious Italian artist from the 60s who died of over-eating when he was only 31 and who did a lot of outrageous Conceptual art things that relied on a recurring gag of the artists' signature, including signing the bodies of naked women and signing cans of his own shit. Robert Morris is a dreary New York artist who used to be good, and was one of the inventors of Minimalism. Duchamp you know.

Once Gavin Turk was in a performance at one of Joshua Compston's art fêtes in Hoxton Square, called *A Fête Worse Than Death*. He recycled David Bowie's song, *Scary Monsters*. He mimed the words on stage, while excreting a string of real sausages from an artificial bottom. Also he recycled Andy Warhol's last self-portraits, which were self-portraits with a camouflage pattern, by photographing himself with the same kind of pattern but giving the photo a title that was a quote from Joseph Conrad's *Heart of Darkness*, which was a bit obscure. Although the same reference is in T. S. Eliot's footnotes to *The Wasteland*, and another thing Gavin Turk tried to recycle was *The Hollow Men* but Faber and Faber wouldn't let him.

Another time he recycled Warhol in another way, which was to have a life-size fibreglass sculpture made of himself dressed like Sid Vicious in the *My Way* section of Julian Temple's film *The Great Rock'n'Roll Swindle*, but posed like Warhol's famous photo of Elvis Presley holding a gun.

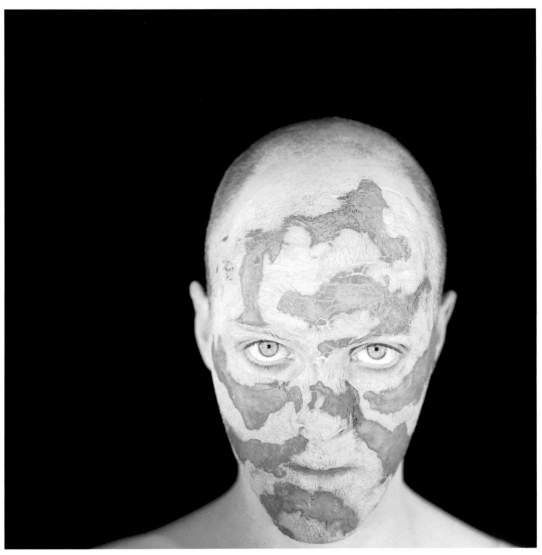

Gavin Turk *Camouflage Self-Portrait (A Man Like Mr. Kurtz)* 1994

Gavin Turk

All this introverted art referencing must have tired him out because until the other day, when he exhibited a realistic skip painted black, which he'd had made by a factory, he seemed to be keeping a low profile. And this skip isn't recycling anything, unless it's an oblique reference to recycling in general, which it might well be of course.

Martin Creed and Owadda

Martin Creed does updated systems art. Systems art was a dry abstract quasi scientific style from the 60s which has returned in the 90s in a loopy form. He does systems music too, with the bassist Kako Owadda, who used to play in my band, Interspecies Love Child. Martin Creed's band is called Owadda after Kako's surname. Which is right on, and multiculturalist, because Kako is Japanese as well as being a woman.

One day a letter came to my house, and when I opened it, it was a screwed up ball of A4 typing paper. And that was a work by Martin Creed. Then another day another letter came, a piece of typing paper torn into little pieces. And that was another work by him.

Abigail Lane

A top artist. She has done many different works including some glass eyeballs on wires in a vitrine, a life-size hyper-realistic sculpture of Angus Fairhurst lying on the floor naked except for an anorak, and many light blue monoprints of a woman's bottom, using the bottom of a woman called Judith.

At the time of John Cage there was a theme of Time and Space in the air, it was the *Zeitgeist* for a while, and a lot of art was roughly about that. One of the equivalent themes now is the body. The body is a site of identity, we go around thinking. So that's a good tip whenever you see any art with bodies or body parts nowadays. Whether it's Abigail Lane's bottoms or her photos of dogs, or just any art featuring bodies or animals, or even just relating somehow, however obliquely, to bodies and the body's activities.

Abigail Lane *Bottom Wallpaper* 1992

top: **Martin Creed**
bottom: **Martin Creed** and **Kako Owadda**

Abigail Lane

Monte Carlo

Many of the young artists now have large well-lit apartments in the East End that were formerly warehouse spaces. In Abigail Lane's space she often puts on avant-garde parties. A regular Friday session features the hairdresser Guy Healey, who cuts all the artists' hair. Afterwards they get a certificate designed to look like a famous photo-montage from the 1920s by Marcel Duchamp called *Monte Carlo Bond*, which related to his ideas about the role of chance in art. *Monte Carlo Bond* was a gambling system that Duchamp evolved. With it, he said, you could neither win nor lose. The original image included a photo of Duchamp with his hair lathered in soap suds with some of the hair shaped into points, like the horns of the Devil. The hairdressing parody you get at Abigail Lane's salons shows herself and Guy Healey, instead of Duchamp, with shampooed hair. I don't know what any of these things mean but they all seem good for a few minutes and the body theme is in there somewhere. Also, she wears a T-shirt that says Complete Arthole, a reference to Sarah Lucas and Tracey Emin's T-shirts. And another party she put on starred a hired-in theatrical company called The Great Stromboli, which featured fire-eating and razor-blade swallowing.

Peter Doig

A figurative painter. He was nominated for the Turner Prize once, and all the young artists like his paintings even though they are well done and you have to scratch your head and frown to see where the irony is.

I saw him walking through the Braque exhibition at the Royal Academy the other day. Braque's paintings have a lot of scumblings of different mixtures of oil paint, and so do Peter Doig's. He mainly does multi-layered, carefully constructed landscape scenes, on a large scale,

Peter Doig *Telemarker (Pas de Chèvres)* 1995–96

with fir trees and snow and people with skis, wearing jackets and hats. At first they seem jolly but sometimes they turn out to be based on film stills, from violent horror films like *Friday 13th* or *The Texas Chainsaw Massacre*. He comes from Canada and often wears rugged lumberjack or ski-style gear himself.

His own explosions

Unpleasant

The art galleries all have a similar style, whether they're in the West or East End and whether they're in an artists' studio or someone's front room. You go in, nobody talks to you, you look around and leave. Unless you're a critic or a collector, in which case someone will come and suck up to you a bit unpleasantly.

Gallery psycho-geographies

Cork Street used to be the main gallery street. Then it had a financial crash in 1990 and was bleak and never recovered, and even Queens, the good old café where everyone used to go, closed. Recently new galleries have been building on the ruins. There is Stephen Friedman and the Entwhistle Gallery, both showing young art.

The Mayor Gallery

But Cork Street will never be the same as it was. Not that it was that good anyway, in fact it was pretty horrible. God, the Mayor Gallery, where they show old bits of Pop Art from the storerooms every now and then. What film do they think they're in, in there? They really do wear pinstripe business suits and smoke cigars and have dead-eyed zombie Sloanes sitting at the reception desk. The gallery featured in an episode of Absolutely Fabulous once, with Joanna Lumley at one point hissing, Can the attitude darling, you're only a shop assistant.

Anthony d'Offay

There are some other galleries nearby in Davies Street, Duke Street and Dering Street. Anthony d'Offay's several gallery spaces are in Dering Street. Anthony d'Offay is dark and pale with a vampire air. He goes back many decades, and he used to show Wyndham Lewis – who invented Vorticism, a little known British art movement from the time of the First World War – and Sir William Coldstream. But gradually he came to be more associated with high-class international up-to-date art like Gilbert & George.

In the past there was a belief that the gallery staff, following his lead, and that of his wife Anne Seymour, who used to work for the Tate Gallery, all did rebirthing, which is a kind of personality therapy involving a ritual where the participants lie in a bath and get reborn. Even if it's true, what's so bad about it? This is a great gallery, where they almost always have good shows of established stars.

What galleries look like

We imagine that galleries are gleaming white cubes but in reality they mostly look like old-fashioned tea-rooms or bespoke tailors or jewellers. Like a Mary Poppins or Upstairs Downstairs world of fake old-style poshness. Collectors seem to like it.

The Marlborough Gallery

The Marlborough Gallery, where they look after Francis Bacon's paintings, is in Albemarle Street, but there's never any reason to go there. I went there recently by accident and there was an exhibition of Christopher LeBrun. He was a neo-Expressionist star of the early 80s. He painted flying horses and was bought by the Saatchis but then he seemed to drift away.

He was taught at the Slade school by Bernard Cohen, who used to do cool pure formal abstract paintings in the 60s, where he would just spray a few coloured dots and some lines, and it would be accepted as a serious painting. That was a definite style in the 60s, but now you never hear about it or him either. Although you sometimes see his paintings at Waddington's and they're quite good.

Leslie Waddington

Leslie Waddington is still there in Cork Street. There's no particular style associated with his gallery. He always seemed like the richest dealer. At the height of the art boom of the 1980s, a new Waddington's would open every few weeks, and every other gallery in Cork Street was called Waddington's. But now there's only two or three. Waddington himself has curly hair and is feared as a tyrant, which is only right for a big gallery boss and we mustn't start judging him without knowing the full story.

It's great when he just pops out of his office into the gallery space and goes up to students and alarms them, and tells them what the paintings mean and how he knew the artist and what masking tape they used. When I was interviewing him once he said he felt the really hot scandal of the 80s was the way drug money was being laundered through the artworld, but the scandal never broke so maybe it's not true.

In the past, Waddington's and d'Offay's never showed new young artists, only established old ones, but now they do. Waddington's shows the ones we were talking about earlier, in connection with warehouse exhibitions, and d'Offay's is always coming up with young surprises.

The Lisson Gallery

Further west is the Lisson Gallery, in Lisson Grove, run by Nicholas Logsdail. This is the only gallery which can really claim to have once had a group of artists that was actually known by the name of the gallery.

Lisson Gallery sculpture was sculpture by Richard Wentworth, Richard Deacon, Bill Woodrow, Tony Cragg, Anish Kapoor and Julian Opie. That was in the early 80s. In the early 90s, when those stars had faded, or at least become so familiar and normal that they weren't thought about much any more, Logsdail tried to scoop up a huge handful of the new young London artists who hadn't yet been scooped up by anyone else, in a single huge group show called 'Wonderful Life'. Hardly anyone wasn't in it.

But then after that, a lot of the young artists who thought they would now be regular Lisson Gallery artists, found they weren't sure if they really were Lisson Gallery artists, because Logsdail had a special knack of making them feel a bit insecure. So some of them just went to other galleries instead and somehow the magic spell of the Lisson Gallery was felt to have been broken.

Tony Cragg *Postcard Union Jack* 1981

But it still remains one of the really powerful galleries, with a strong voodoo magic lingering on. And to show there is a very important step, and Logsdail himself is still a greatly respected figure for having not only been

Nicholas Logsdail

in at the beginning of Conceptual art in the 60s and 70s, but for being one of the best-known dealers of the international art boom of the 80s too.

Winston Churchill

As he grew older, Logsdail became more and more eccentric and started going around with his glasses half way down his nose and peering over the top of them and holding his arms out at you and saying, How are you my boy? like Winston Churchill.

Explosions

In the East End there is Interim Art in Beck Road. Beck Road is an artists' street because all the houses in it are run by Acme. Acme itself is further out in Bow or somewhere. It used to be in Covent Garden, and it had its own gallery, the Acme Gallery, where Kerry Trengove once dug a tunnel in the 70s, under the ground and out into the street, which

INTERIM ART

took a week to do. And Stuart Brisley starved himself for ten days over Christmas, while an uneaten Christmas dinner rotted horribly around him. And Bruce Lacey installed himself and his wife and goats in the gallery, so that it was an artist-hippie commune for a while, with a hole in the roof to let the stars shine through. And the Kipper Kids did their performances there. They would drink their own urine. And then one of them went to America and married Bette Midler. There was an amazing explosions artist of the 70s called Steve Cripps who showed at Acme too, but he sadly died in one of his own explosions.

More East End

Matt's Gallery, run by Robin Klassnick, the first pioneer gallerist to open up in the East End, is in the present Acme building in Bow, but it used to be in Space Studios, near Interim Art, in Hackney. Space is the same as Acme, supplying subsidized studio spaces for artists, only smaller. It was started in the 60s by a collective that included Bridget Riley.

There used to be a whole artists' sub-culture in Wapping in the 70s but they had to move in the early 80s, because it was all developed round there. Now it's just that strange abandoned yuppie development zone.

Interim Art

Maureen Paley's private views at Interim Art are on Sunday afternoons. She is always starkly black and white, or black, white and grey, with a white face and black hair with extensions, which she has had since the 80s. Although probably by now it's her real hair. Don't be frightened, you feel like saying whenever you see her. Because she always looks a bit afraid. But in reality she has led a bold life, opening a gallery in the East End at a very early stage, the early 80s, before it was fashionable to do that, and keeping going for all this time.

More West End

There are a handful of galleries on the Interim Art level, which is medium to low money, but high critical credibility, in the West End. Some of these cluster around Foley Street, off Tottenham Court Road. For example,

Laure Genillard. Karsten Schubert used to be there but he closed down in a fit of pique when Rachel Whiteread left him for Anthony d'Offay. Nearby there are some newer galleries. Lotta Hammer in Cleveland Road and Robert Prime in Warren Street. It's great that all those galleries are run by foreigners. Another one is Victoria Miro on Cork Street. But she's English, I think.

Superstars

To open a gallery you need some backing, because it's expensive, but you don't need to be an intellectual. That's just a social thing they all do. A way of talking that they copy from their artists, who mostly aren't really intellectual either. People who run galleries are just like anyone else running a business. But the bigger or more critically attended to the gallery is, the more afflicted by superstar psychosis the gallerist is likely to be.

High
all the time

Art magazines

This is the mystery section. No ordinary person would ever read most art magazines because they're in a completely secret language. But the ones that are in ordinary language, and there are some, don't have anything to say. That's the mystery, the way art criticism now can only be real if it's secret, even though it's nothing like the other secret worlds, science or psychology or philosophy, say.

Artworld people say, What do you mean you can't understand art talk? Would you expect to understand the talk of a nuclear physicist? Don't you see that art is a special subject like that, you have to do some work at it! But in reality people in the artworld mostly just think moronic thoughts like everyone else, and it's nothing like nuclear physics.

Artscribe is the magazine I used to edit. Then it folded. *Frieze*, which is always spelt in lower case, *frieze*, but not *freeze*, like the warehouse exhibition, is for young people. That's the most important one.

Art Monthly, the oldest one, has gradually become more and more for young people, but some old people probably go on still subscribing, not realizing there's nothing in it for them any more. Soon there's going to be a massive return of the repressed artworld old people.

In the 60s and 70s the most important magazine in the London artworld, apart from *Artforum* which was imported from New York, was *Studio International*. That was edited by Peter Townsend, who is a journalist who had famously been to China in the 1930s, when nobody else went there. In fact I think he was called Townsend of China, like Gordon of Khartoum.

After *Studio International* he helped put together *Art Monthly*, which was founded in about 1976, with the American expatriate Jack Wendler whose family made money from vending machines I think, unless that's a rhyming association with Wendler, and who used to run a Conceptual art gallery in the 60s, or was a Conceptual art dealer or organizer or something. Both him and his wife Nell Wendler still work on *Art Monthly* and you see them both at private views. The editor now is Patricia Bickers because Peter Townsend went to Australia and founded *Australian Art*

Monthly. But he seems to have come back recently because I sometimes see him on the bus.

How to read them

Art magazines are for art professionals. The way they're consumed is that they are rapidly flicked through to see if the user's name or the names of any friends are mentioned. Then the ads are read. Then the rest is gradually browsed through. The pictures, the captions, the first few lines of the articles. Then gradually the reviews are read because even if you're not mentioned they're short and the pain is less.

These magazines are so vital, it's amazing. It's a relief to go on holiday for a while and not see any. But you soon get hooked again. What the hell are you looking for? you ask yourself after a while.

Carl Freedman is good

When *frieze* started out, the writing was quite undistinguished, they were just mopping up the left-overs from the other magazines. But now it's got a few regular names and you look out for them. Carl Freedman is good. He was one of the journalists who had to nail the million pounds to a board for the K Foundation, for their obscure anti-money event. He pocketed £1,600 and was amazed that none of the other journalists, who were from ordinary papers, thought of doing the same. But that's mainstream journalism for you!

Conflict

Modern Painters was started by Peter Fuller, who died in 1990 in a motorway accident. In the last years of his life he was a very well known public figure, always on TV and in the papers. In those days he stood for a creepy kind of neo-Conservatism and was always going on about how good Prince Charles was. But when he first became widely known in the artworld, in the mid 70s, he was an energetic Marxist, always shouting and sputtering in public art seminars against capitalism. He thought everything he couldn't understand, like almost all contemporary art, was capitalism.

Carl Freedman

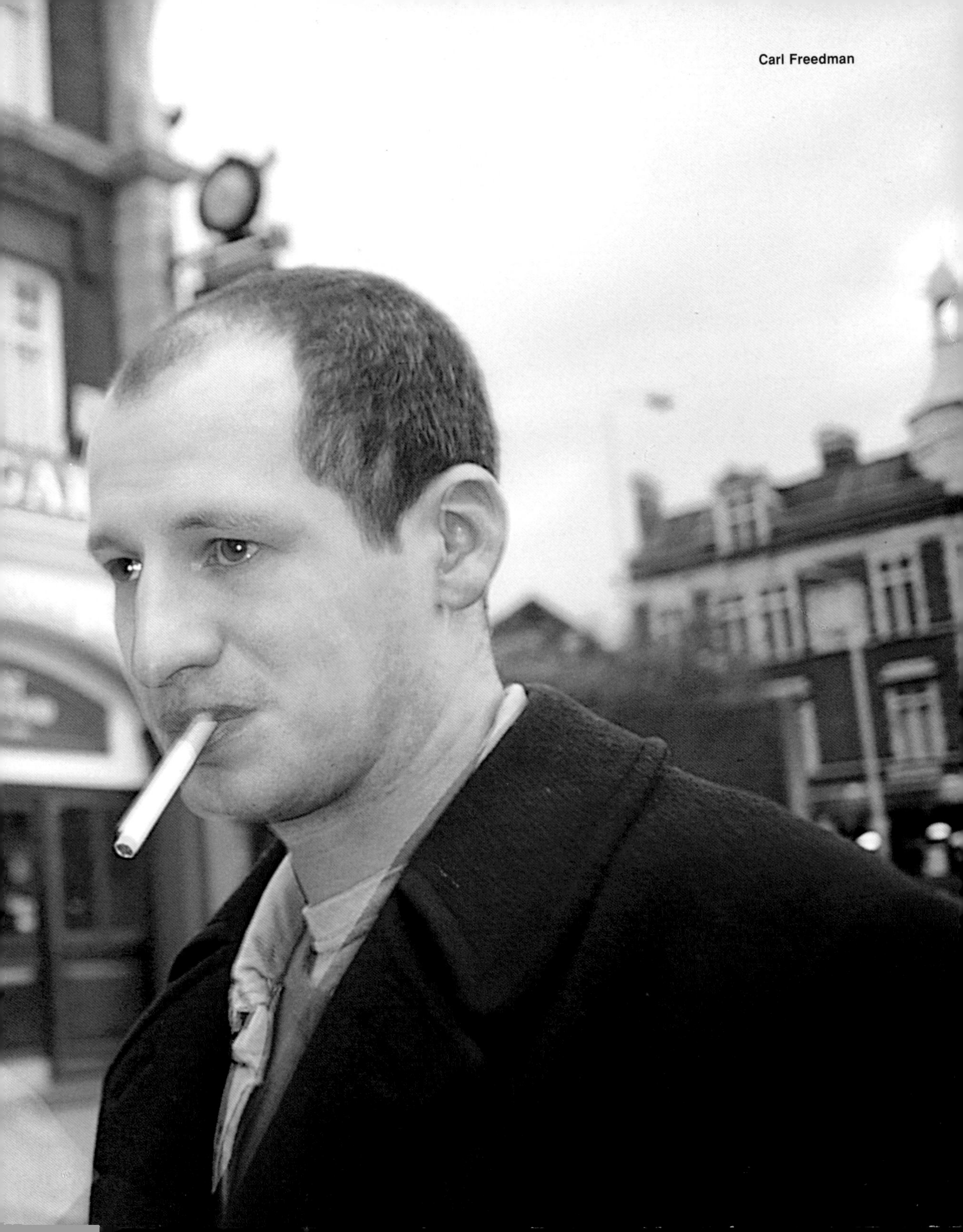

He was addicted to gambling and had to have psychoanalysis for twelve years at the Anna Freud Institute. His father had been a minister and he would often embarrass the young Peter Fuller in public by not being able to understand how ordinary people behaved, how they ordered a meal in a restaurant for example.

When I met him, it was for an interview in *Artscribe*. I instantly liked him and thought he was funny. I didn't care about his writing being so ghastly. In conversation it was like he was high all the time. He was very honest about his own personality and his power-madness and the conflicts that drove him and he made quite good jokes against himself.

Then I didn't see him again for a while and then he was in a pilot for a BBC discussion programme which never made it onto the air. In the hospitality room afterwards we were talking and I mentioned how weird it was that everything he liked nobody cared about, like Henry Moore and so on. And he said I was wrong and actually there was a huge audience for that kind of thing, and it turned out he was right, as *Modern Painters* seems to keep on going.

Postbox

Stuart Morgan is a legendary figure of the London artworld. All artists want him to write their catalogues and review their shows. He often supports quite odd artists that you don't hear about again after he's written about them, and that's another plus, because it means he doesn't just follow the herd.

He can be very funny. His articles were rounded up and published in a book recently. The best one was about Jerry Lewis's 24-hour telethons in the 1970s, when Jerry Lewis used to raise money for spastic children by really outrageous and embarrassing egotistical behaviour, which did actually result in millions of dollars being sent in. Like the event itself, the article seems to be coming from all sorts of different directions so you don't know whether to laugh or cry, and although it's hard to say in what way it connects to art, somehow it seems to. And that's why he's good generally.

He never seemed to have anywhere to live. Once in the 80s I saw him late at night alone in Brick Lane clutching a box of Kentucky Fried Chicken and I felt a bit sad, because obviously he was sleeping on someone's floor and meals weren't included. Another time he was sleeping in a spare room in my flat in Stoke Newington for a few nights, but the Polish Conceptual artist Piotr Nathan kept sleeping in there with him. And after he left, postcards kept arriving from Poland, with a message in broken English at the top. Sorry to use you as postbox Matthew.

Plastic bag

Tim Hilton writes for the *Sunday Independent*, and is a very elegant writer. He really does have a mind of his own and always goes against the grain, preferring old fashioned painters to new young trendy art. But at the same time he always seems a bit angry and perhaps deliberately keeps himself a bit out of touch with now. So you feel a bit suspicious about some of his judgements about the artists of now. He keeps up a good Bohemian appearance though, and goes around very dishevelled with a red face and carrying a plastic bag, with sandwiches in it perhaps.

Compelling

Sarah Kent is the editor of *Time Out*'s visual arts section. There are six or seven weekly reviews, done by herself and a team of other writers. Every week she finds a new young artist to come out fighting for. Briliant! the review will end. In fact that's become the house style now. Brilliant! they all end. Or, Compelling!

Colour

Patrick Heron, the main St Ives painter, now an old man, is a writer too. He used to write for the *New Statesman* in the 50s and 60s and was always campaigning against realism. He thought abstraction was better. He still pops up today and just writes about colour in an incredibly passionate and unapologetic way. It's very boring for ordinary people and even for most artists, but I think it's great.

Brian Sewell

A natural entertainer with a good act. No one knows what really drives him.

Do not film my plimsolls

Wow! The best art writer of all. David Sylvester. *Interviews with Francis Bacon*, that was his book. He had an article published in the *The Guardian* recently about Gilbert & George, comparing them to the best that the Renaissance had to offer. This was in connecton with their exhibition called 'The Naked Shit Pictures'. In the margin in bold type was an editorial note saying he is the most important art critic in the world.

And it's true, he just has gravitas, there's no way around it. He turned up for a *Late Show* interview at the Hayward Gallery once, very early in the morning, about the Magritte exhibition he had organized there, and immediately launched into a terrifying onslaught, with the most amazing swearing, out of nowhere. And it took a long time for me to realize the BBC was the target, and not me personally. I think. I was hoping anyway.

He was saying the BBC didn't take him seriously and they treated him like a cunt and he could make his own fucking films about Magritte. And it was true he had actually made one, in the 60s or 70s, or some time like that. But the remarkable thing was how contained this Tourette's tornado was, and how after it was over he just did the interview in his usual dignified style as if nothing really incredibly weird had just happened. He was wearing plimsolls. Do not film my plimsolls, he said.

Malcolm Morley, the voice and the myth

David Sylvester is a great champion of the artist Malcolm Morley. He compares him to the greatest of the Dutch realists of the seventeenth century, and to de Kooning, because that's the kind of art critic he is.

Malcolm Morley doesn't figure very largely, or even at all, in the new London artworld, since he has lived in America since 1958. Nevertheless, he is one of the great products of the London artworld, a larger than life character who it would be hard to believe really existed if he didn't keep popping up and frightening people like he does.

Malcolm Morley

He has a reputation for irrascibility but his main significance is that he seems to stick to an incredibly old-fashioned idea of painting. That it should look like something, be bright and pleasurable, full of light, show a lot of wrist action, and not have a lot of extraneous theories or mystification going on. But he found an avant-garde way of doing this and his paintings never look normal even though they are full of normal pleasures and you can't help liking them.

Over the years a mythology has grown up around him, the result of his infrequent but always fantastically vivid and entertaining interviews. He said his painting method was method acting. He did hyper-ventilating and read a lot and was in psychoanalysis for many years. When he was young during the war, his house was bombed and his model aeroplanes all broke, and models and disasters and war have been constant themes in his paintings. When a painting of his was being re-sold at auction once, he shot it with a water pistol filled with paint, which was quite violent of him, and illegal, as it was no longer his to shoot.

A wandering star

He was born under a wandering star. When he was young he wandered to America on an ocean liner, about the time R.B.Kitaj was wandering in the opposite direction, from America to London. And when he got there he painted abstract straight lines at first, and then he invented photo-realism.

Photo-realism took off and dominated the artworld for four years. Which was about as long as classic Cubism lasted in the early 1900s. That's the kind of point he would make and you would think, Hmm, that's interesting. Although in fact Cubism lasted about eight years, didn't it?

His photo-realism paintings were realistic copies of photos of ocean liners mostly. Then he stopped doing that and started making his realistic paintings all strange and fragmented, with the photo-based imagery disturbed by nervous expressionist brushstrokes. He said Cézanne spoke to him in the shower and told him to paint like that.

His paintings became more and more spatially complicated, and the imagery he favoured – images of travel – started to become violent and weird, full of catastrophes and accidents. He had been a student at Camberwell art school before he went to live in America. But before that he was a criminal and had been in Wormwood Scrubs for three years, where he learned to paint landscapes from a correspondence course.

In a way, when he started being a neo-Expressionist, which is what he was in the mid-70s, his ocean liners and aeroplanes and toy soldiers all exploding with phallic imagery and polymorphous perversion (which is a concept from Freud, which the writer Norman O. Brown made intellectually trendy in the 60s), it was as if it was the return of the repressed Camberwell loose painting style.

He always sold everything he did, from an early stage, and nowadays he's one of the world's most expensive living artists. He said culture rewards repression, referring to his incredibly slow working method.

He certainly does paint in a very repressed way, covering the canvas inch by inch, maybe only filling up a few inches a day, and using the old-fashioned pencil grids that artists since the Renaissance have used to get an image accurately copied.

Malcolm Morley
Erotic Blando Fruto: La Mariposa 1988–89

His source material nowadays is not photos but water-colours which he does himself, with free loose marks, of fishing boats in the Caribbean and mangoes and bananas and planes and hot air balloons. When he transposes them onto canvas, using his traditional grid technique, every blob and splash of the watercolour becomes a dramatic painterly incident in the oil painting.

Unpleasantness alert

When Malcolm Morley won the first Turner Prize, which caused a lot of resentment because he didn't live in Britain, I interviewed him for *Artscribe*, at the Savoy hotel where he was staying. During the interview his old mother phoned up, who he hadn't seen since he was a child. He wasn't brought up by her. She had seen him on TV and phoned the Tate Gallery and they gave her his number at the Savoy. That's the sort of mythic thing that happens to him.

The interview went well after I compared him to de Kooning. I only did that because I'd met him the night before at a de Kooning opening, and it came into my head, even though they're not very similar at all. After that I didn't see him for a few years. Then I had to go and interview him again, this time at the Anthony d'Offay Gallery for a TV programme. Unfortunately that was a disaster and it ended very unpleasantly. He was behaving like a monster art brat, even though he was in his sixties, being really awkward about giving his interview, and after a while I said, Look I'm not an idiot. And he said, in his mid-Atlantic cockney Long Island accent, No, but you're an arsehole.

David Sylvester was there and as I was leaving, white-faced, he looked all mournful with his deep-set brown eyes, like they were filled with all the sadness in the world. And then he kindly stepped in and took over the interview, asking his gravitas questions, with the good theatrical pauses that are actually quite unnerving for contemporary TV, with Malcolm Morley answering more or less OK now. But in the end the film wasn't shown.

War of the worlds

TV programmes about art are a mystery to the artworld. People in the artworld wonder why what they go around thinking in their heads isn't the content of art programmes. Why does it have to be what's in the TV producer's head? No one can solve the riddle. But you can torture yourself needlessly about these things. When I worked on *The Late Show*, artists would come up and say, Hey, *The Late Show* is really bad. But then after they'd been on it they'd say, Hey, *The Late Show* is getting better. And they'd really mean it and not see the connection.

Richard Hamilton is civilized

We sometimes think TV films about art have got better and better because they're more up-to-date in their style now. But the most up-to-date ones were in the 60s when it was Richard Hamilton on *Monitor* interviewing Marcel Duchamp or Tingueley. He just asked them things in a civilized way and they answered, and if you were lucky there was a bit of film of them making some art. It was straightforward and you could hardly tell it was TV at all.

Stop whispering

There was a series in the early 80s called *State of the Art* which was meant to be an updating of all the latest artworld attitudes. But it was very difficult to feel at ease with that series because although it had really up-to-date attitudes, it also had a made-up sound track of whispering voices done by actors, which was supposed to be a metaphor for the many voices of Post-Modernism, and that was quite embarrassing.

Drank the finger bowl

Last night I dreamed I was writing an article about Charles Saatchi and I was ticking off all the points about him that I had to remember on a list and one point said, Drank the finger bowl. The time I drank the finger bowl was when I was meeting the Saatchis, Charles and Doris, in a Japanese restaurant in the mid 80s, to beg them to buy *Artscribe* and get us out of debt. They showed me how to use chopsticks and then when the finger bowl arrived I drank it. As soon as I'd done it, I knew it was probably wrong, but they were kind enough not to say anything, and maybe even drank their finger bowls too.

Charles Saatchi

In those days Charles Saatchi looked like the one press photo of him that was always used in the papers, even though it had probably been taken in 1975. Curly dark hair, bland smile, straight-looking suit and tie. Then suddenly later on he started looking good, wearing designer clothes, and that's been his look ever since. A hedonist millionaire suntanned designer groovy guy.

The Tate Gallery

They didn't buy *Artscribe* after all, partly because someone at the Tate Gallery told them not to. Thanks Tate Gallery! But also partly because they wisely decided it might be bad for the credibility of an art magazine to be owned by the collectors of the art that the magazine was mainly featuring.

Guilty

Later on when I was unemployed, I would bump into Saatchi occasionally and he was always very supportive and would say encouraging things like, What are you going to do now? Why don't you open a gallery? But then I was working at the BBC, and a job I had there quite early on was to write the commentary for a short film about Saatchi's art collecting, and after that he never spoke to me again. And of course I felt guilty, although at the same time I couldn't understand what the film had said that was so bad. He just doesn't like anything to be said about him that isn't incredibly bland praise. When people are like that we kind of roll our eyes a bit. But if it was us, of course, we'd feel the same.

Nuclear

And really you have to admit he's been an amazing force in the London artworld. At this moment the whole thing more or less depends on him. He just goes round all the shows buying them up. In other countries there are lots of medium energy collectors and one or two really huge, high energy ones. But in this country there are very few collectors and almost all of them are low energy except for him. He is nuclear energy. The other countries' art scenes depend on the middle ground of medium collectors, whereas over here we depend only on him. All the young artists go around scratching their heads and wondering what would happen if he just stopped doing it. Would the curators at the Tate Gallery go around buying all that stuff, or the BBC, or the Arts Council, or the Queen, or Sting? No. Hey, the young artists would be broke!

How many Lucian Freuds

The last conversation I had with Saatchi was on the phone all those years ago, at the time the film was being made and the papers were all carrying the story about him selling off huge numbers of Anselm Kiefers and Julian Schnabels and Sigmar Polkes for the millions of pounds they were worth in those days, before the market for them went down. And he was really furious that the papers should be going on about that, and he thought everyone should say what a lot of good he had done, and point out how many Lucian Freuds he'd bought. And if they kept on complaining, he said, he would close his gallery, which was for the general public, and buy a yacht and be selfish and just behave like a normal millionaire.

Shy

Then one year he made the Turner Prize award speech and he said Young British art might be vulgar sometimes but then aren't we all sometimes. And that's a point of some kind.

People often ask why he does all that buying. Is he an intellectual or just a speculator? He always keeps up a mysterious shy profile, never giving interviews or appearing in public, except now and then as an exception, to prove the rule and keep the mystery fresh. But I think we can discount shy. He clearly is a speculator. But an enthusiast too. After all, you can be more than one thing in this life.

No, he is not an intellectual as far as I've noticed. But God, is that such a crime? He has the normal art collector character. But on a bigger scale. He wants to be talked about and be associated with something that is indefinable and mysterious and glamorous, and not just crass like yachts or movies. And he probably gets a kick out of frightening the art dealers, and lording it over them, but then that's their problem, they don't have to do that job.

And now

And now he's bought nearly all the Chapmans' disturbing children mannequins. And apparently also practically the whole of the Martin Maloney show, 'Die Yuppie Scum', as a job lot, which means in a way he's kind of bought the mind of a writer, which is a strange idea, and there seems no end to his buying.

Soon, it's rumoured, he's going to open a gallery in New York, like his one in St John's Wood. When he does that New York will be able to see the new London art in the flesh straight away, instead of after the event in magazines. And it will be an unexpected reversal of the old days, when the artists over here longed to see New York art straight away so they could copy it, and then suddenly in about 1957 it was over here *en masse* and we were overwhelmed and it never went away and it took about 40 years for us to come up with our own stuff. Now we won't be caring about Jackson Pollock or Schnabel or Sean Landers any more, and they'll all be caring about Marc Quinn and Bob and Roberta Smith and Gillian Wearing instead.

So Charles Saatchi really is the single most powerful force in the rise of British art, more than any artist. I don't think there can really be any question about that.

On the escalator

Leon Kossoff *Booking Hall, Kilburn Underground Station No. 2* 1977

Spasmodic

Elizabeth Wright is a young artist who does ordinary objects out of scale, like 50 per cent reduced office furniture, or enlarged cigarette butts. Or a perfect *Evening Standard* that's only a few inches wide. Or the Zurich telephone directory, also only a few inches wide. But tonight at the Showroom Gallery in Hackney she's showing a full-scale corner of a new house, perfectly made, which she has had designed by an architect. It looks really startling.

I'm talking to Simon Martin who paints abstract squares, and Gary Hume, who's wearing red sunglasses, and I'm handing out invitation cards to a benefit exhibition which will be at my studio next week. All the works in this show, which have been donated to the exhibition, will be on sale for £50 each, regardless of who made them, whether it's Adam Chodzko or someone you've never heard of. That's why the exhibition is called 'Fifty Quid'. It's to raise money to pay the rates on the studio.

Anyway, Say you'd earned something one week, I'm saying to Simon Martin – who does in fact regularly sign on – And you have to sign off. Are you supposed to not sign on again until the money's run out, or can you just sign on again the next week, regardless of what the amount was? What if it was £1,000, say, for an article?

Gary Hume is keeping quiet, I suppose because he earns so much now it's not an issue. But earlier he was being very nice and saying it's a shame I haven't been on TV for a while. Which is a change from how he can sometimes be, when he is being drunk and scary, like when he asked about the spaces between my teeth, once, at a dinner party. Or when he had a very realistic gun, maybe it even was real, at one of Joshua Compston's modern art fêtes in Hoxton Square one year, and he was firing it at the ground in front of me. Or when he was at the party after a Gilbert & George opening and he was psyching me out by pushing his face into mine and it was kind of spasmodically jerking as if he was in a horror film and a demon had entered his body. But I think a lot of this is just nerves.

At the back of the gallery there's a table with a display of photo-copied documents which turn out to be the results of a government survey

Elizabeth Wright *Untitled* 1996

about ideal housing which was conducted in the late 40s I think. That's a bit disturbing, because it makes the house artwork seem a bit worthy, like a social statement, and perhaps reduces the startling surrealism effect of it being inside a gallery space.

But then I see Rachel Whiteread sitting by the window in a row of artists drinking beers, and I realize it's better this way because it would seem too much like her concrete house, even though it's nothing like that. But if you went around saying, Oh Elizabeth Wright's done a house, people would immediately think, Oh Rachel Whiteread. Also, it's good to combine surrealism and documentarism.

Everyone looks baffled when I say I'm going to the Tate Gallery to a Leon Kossoff private view.

Smock shock

When I get there it's towards the end of the private view. Unlike the Showroom show, where everyone was dressed normally, everyone here is dressed horribly in navy blue suits, both the men and the women. Except for one or two who are in laughable artist costumes, though no one's laughing. Light blue artists' smocks and sandals and white beards.

The two main social groups are, firstly, the really startling nutty inbred braying young and old fogies that every now and then you encounter *en masse*, and realize, with a shudder, that these are the ones who actually rule the world, and the artworld too. And who the Tate Gallery always hires from some kind of agency for all their private views. And secondly the family and friends of the artist, who are the only normal people.

Leon Kossoff is a painter in his seventies who does a kind of Existential horror painting, with the figures all looming and staring, like they've just seen a ghost, and the brown and grey paint all spattering and bulging, and the colour all drained out, so there's no danger of feeling happy. Dalston Lane, Willesden Junction, Kilburn Underground, Spitalfields Church. He makes the normal London landscape come alive in a weird way.

One painting from the 70s shows four figures who look like they're from *Night of the Evil Dead*, looking for human flesh to eat, spread out in the ticket office at Kilburn underground. And in the background you can see those strange tall blue box-shape things they used to have on the underground, with a big 30p sign on them, on a bright patch of yellow, where you got your tickets. The label says this picture is owned by Summit Hotels Bel Air and Beverley Hills.

Polystyrene

Exmouth Market off Rosebery Avenue. I've left the Tate Gallery now and I'm at another private view which is being held in nine empty shops in this street. Each one is a temporary gallery while the owner waits to find buyers for the spaces. One has some polystyrene cups in a row in a vitrine, by Christina Mackie. The cups have been subjected to varying degrees of super-powered hot-air pressure, from being put in a micro-wave or something. So one is normal, whereas the others are shrunk, from slightly less than normal size to very small. Another gallery has a

Christina Mackie
Suppression, Repression,
Depression, Compression
1995

film of an empty room projecting on the back wall, which is a live outside-broadcast from an artist's studio, with nothing at all going on in it.

The artists are hanging around outside in the street, where cars are forbidden to go. Andrew Wilson is there, with another topic for this book. Artists' assistants and drug dealers. Apparently Robert Fraser who ran the famous Robert Fraser gallery in the 60s and who is the man handcuffed to Mick Jagger in Richard Hamilton's famous print, and who re-opened his gallery in Cork Street in the the 80s but then sadly died of AIDS, used to share the same heroin dealer with Alexander Trocchi. But now it's the next day and that's the only drug dealer example I can remember and I don't think the assistants idea has any mileage.

Artists' assistants

The Chapman brothers were Gilbert & George's assistants. And Anthony Caro was Henry Moore's. Liam Gillick was Michael Craig Martin's. Marc Quinn was Barry Flanagan's. I can't see a pattern emerging yet.

Will it last?

This is often the question about art today. Will it last? Will we still think it's good in 50 years? But really there's no answer. Or, even if the answer is no, so what? The good thing about art is that it isn't government funded, at least not very much, so it basically comes from an underground culture but it's still a high art form. That's good, to be high and underground at the same time.

Staring and blinking

When you see Gilbert & George now they look quite old and their suits and haircuts don't seem odd on them, like they used to. In those days everyone wore flairs and had long hair and sideburns, so Gilbert & George stuck out. One thing we forget is how they used to be not just visually very striking but actually quite beautiful, especially in their films. They had a silent cinema appeal, like Louise Brooks.

Two of their films were on the other day at Anthony d'Offay, from the early 70s, called *In the Bush* and *Portrait of the Artists*.

In grainy black and white, a locked-off camera shows them far away, in a bush in a London park, awkwardly moving around. The sound-track is birds tweeting. That's *In the Bush*. In *Portrait* they're in close-up in an empty white space, with George drinking and Gilbert just staring and blinking.

George is drinking now

George is drinking now. In fact he's been drinking all day and now he's swaying and tilting and slurring his words. We're at a party in their honour at a house in Cambridge, far from the Market Café in Fournier Street where they go each day for their sausages and gravy. Gilbert, with his grey hair and grey suit, is saying, That's just ham don't you think? They're talking about Georg Bazelitz, the German artist. They think German Expressionist painting is the worst art of today.

They like young London art but at the same time they're quite sarcastic about the craze for glossy lifestyle magazine articles on the subject.

When I say I'm photographing about twenty artists for this book they say, Only twenty? And George says dryly, We thought there were 50,000 of them now.

They never used to think about Francis Bacon when they were students because he only did painting. But we like his screams, they say.

Mechanically spinning

Someone phoned up today who had been in New York and seen Damien Hirst's new exhibition at the Larry Gagosian Gallery there, and apparently it reverses all the reservations about his continuing vitality as an artist, which have been running through this book, and is full of upbeat sculptures of giant ashtrays and carnivalesque sections of pigs in locomotion and circular spin paintings that are actually spinning, mechanically, and a cow cut into a lot of crosswise sections instead of down the middle, and all the sections in their own vitrines, so the cow seems to be stretching on for many yards.

Damien Hirst
Gagosian Gallery installation
1996

But then somebody else phoned up and said it was just cynical over-production.

Ho ho

And apparently Saatchi bought this new cow sculpture for $250,000. Which is about the price of a small Jasper Johns drawing. Which I know because I was in a Johns drawing exhibition at Anthony d'Offay's the other day, and someone was trying to buy one and the assistant told him the price but then said they couldn't just sell it to him because they didn't know who he was. And then another assistant came up and asked him where he fitted in, and he said he didn't fit in at all, and they all laughed nervously. But then after a bit more intercourse, including a lot of ho-ho-ing in posh royal family braying, it turned out he did fit in after all, because he was the friend of a regular d'Offay patron, and the bad moment passed.

Quo vadis?

Where are you going, young artists? Are you any use? You're always flying around in jets and being in international group shows and staying in hotels. What do you care what anything means? Wearing your suits in *Vanity Fair*. That's what I was thinking the other day in the Prado in Madrid, in the Velazquez room, with the court dwarves.

Is this the best museum in the world or what? The dwarves are soulful. The peasants are red and grinning. The royals are staring inbredly. Every scene is a marvel. Could we get painting like this back again today? We'd have to get the whole of reality set up in a completely different way and that would be impossible. And all the thought and ideas and literature and culture and beliefs and symbols. We'd have to get them done too.

The other good room is the one with Goya's black paintings, which he painted on the walls of his house when he was old, for only himself to look at. I thought I was in heaven down there, even though it was all processions of mad people and leering grotesque oldsters eating their gruel with wooden spoons. It was the first moment of Existentialism in art. Other people being in hell already in the eighteenth century instead of waiting till the 1950s. They stare out with their mad eyes, playing their flamenco guitars, singing *We'll Meet Again* in Spanish.

And maybe they will. On the escalator with Francis Bacon, who died in Madrid after an asthma attack. Or on that bridge in London in T. S. Eliot's *The Wasteland*. Or in the Market Café. Or in 1990 in the Saatchi Gallery, with those flies.

The Market Café in Fournier Street

Photographic Credits

The publishers have made every effort to contact all holders of copyright works. All copyright holders who we have been unable to reach are invited to write to the publishers so that a full acknowledgement may be given in subsequent editions.

We are very grateful to the artists for their permission to reproduce the works and for agreeing to have their photos taken.

The publishers also wish to thank the owners and photographers of works reproduced in this book for kindly granting permission for their use. Photographs have been provided by owners and those listed below:

Arts Council Collection, Hayward Gallery, London p. 38
Courtesy Beyeler Collection, Basle p. 40
Rory Carnegie/Jay Jopling p. 13
© John Deakins Archive. Courtesy James Moores Collection, London p. 92
Photo by Daniel Farson. Courtesy Marlborough Fine Art, London p. 51
Courtesy Anthony d'Offay Gallery, London p.190
Courtesy Fondation Maeght, pp. 39, 54, 55
Photo by Lee Friedlander, 1984. Courtesy Marlborough Fine Art, London p. 51
Courtesy Gagosian Gallery, New York p. 205
Gilbert & George pp. 57, 59, 62, 63
Courtesy Glenn Scott Wright, London p. 162
Photo Timothy Greenfield-Sanders, 1990 p. 190
Courtesy Lotta Hammer, London p. 132
Photo © Michal Heiman, 1988, Israel. Courtesy Pace Wildenstein, New York p. 11
© David Hockney p. 53
Courtesy Jay Jopling (London) pp. 18, 23, 98, 108, 115, 127, 153, 159
Courtesy Annely Juda Fine Art, London p. 58
Courtesy Lisson Gallery, London pp. 96, 118–119, 120, 121, 122, 123, 143
© Ian MacMillan front and back cover, pp. 5, 25, 28–29, 37, 42, 43, 44–45, 47, 71, 78–79, 81, 82–83, 91, 97, 101, 103–105, 106–107, 109, 111, 116–117, 124–125, 131, 136–137, 140–141, 145, 147, 149, 151, 155, 156–157, 160–161, 163, 164–165, 166, 169, 170–171, 175, 176–177, 181, 184–185, 189, 207
Courtesy Marlborough Fine Art, London p. 114
Courtesy Matt's Gallery, London pp. 84, 86
Courtesy Victoria Miro Gallery, London p. 46, 99, 146, 158, 167
Courtesy MOMA, New York p. 50
Courtesy Maureen Paley/Interim Art, London p. 126
Courtesy October Gallery Trust, London p. 94
Courtesy Andrea Rosen Gallery, New York p. 16
Courtesy The Saatchi Collection, London pp. 14, 19, 85, 102, 103, 138, 139
Courtesy Julian Schnabel p. 11
Courtesy Karsten Schubert, London p. 150
Courtesy The Showroom Gallery, London p. 199
Courtesy Summit Hotels, Bel-Air and Beverley Hills p.197
Courtesy Tate Gallery, London p. 52
Courtesy Waddington Galleries pp. 30, 32, 95
Photo Richard Waite p. 6
Photo Edward Woodman. © Helen Chadwick Estate, London p. 87
Photo Cerith Wyn Evans p. 201
Photo Richard Young/Rex p. 193

Acknowledgements

This book is for beautiful Emma Biggs. I love you. Thank you very much to everyone else who helped me by reading the manuscript and taking out the spelling mistakes, split infinitives and bitter bits. Thank you to everyone I went up to and asked for ideas. Thank you Babette, my daughter, and Rosalind Collings, my beautiful mother. Thank you Susan Shaw. Thank you Clare Beavan, Andrée Cooke, Jackie Pennell and Josephine Pride. Thank you Ian MacMillan for taking such good photos, and Herman Lelie and Stefania Bonelli for the inspired design and setting, and Uwe Kraus for organizing the printing so efficiently. Thank you Linda Saunders and Georgia Mazower for being so thorough. Thank you Karen Wright for being kind and patient. Thank you artists, I'm sorry it can't be like Velazquez again.